THE FREE LUNCH

Fairness with Freedom

D1227466

THE
FREE LUNCH

Fairness with Freedom

Charles Bazlinton

Orchard Four Books

THE FREE LUNCH
© Charles Bazlinton 2002

First published in 2002
Reprinted with corrections & revisions 2003
Reprinted (international cover) 2005

Published by:
Orchard Four Books
PO Box 103
Alresford
SO24 9XN

web: www.the-free-lunch.com

ISBN 0 9544105 0 5

cover: www.dominicstoppani.com

Printed by:

RPM Print & Design, Chichester

To

Peggy,
Sophie, Graeme,
Kate, Claude,
Emma and Dominic with thanks
for their encouragement over the long time
this book took to be written

and

to anyone
who still retains a hope
that there must be a way to loosen
the grip of the Lottery Principle,
despite the many failed attempts so far.

Notes & Acknowledgements

THERE IS A CONUNDRUM about the last 100 years or so. Whilst technological advances have brought some benefit to almost everyone on the planet, the poor are still with us in much greater numbers than earlier visionaries would have expected.

The 20th century subjected the people of dozens of nations to economic experiments. It was assumed that if the state were given the resources, it would succeed in drastically reducing poverty. So why does it still endure, even in wealthy nations in good economic times?

As the economic experiments were starting, Henry George, through his book *Progress and Poverty* made a huge international impact. He clearly understood why poverty endures despite technological advance, and his book explained the remedy. It was also his opinion that socialistic methods: *'the substitution of government direction for the play of individual action, and the attempt to secure by restriction what can better be secured by freedom'*, were not the best way of applying the remedy. He warned of the problems that would arise if that route was followed. This book is partly a modern exploration of his insights which are as fresh and relevant as they were when he wrote them.

The issues discussed are like the many facets of a sculpture that can best be appreciated as the observer moves and brings a slightly different aspect into view. Once the issue has been grasped there is an unexpected simplicity to the answers proposed, but their backgrounds needs explanation and their outcomes need to be inter-related. Apart from some understanding from my surveying background I have relied on the findings of others, as acknowledged in the text, for insights from other disciplines

I would like to thank several people specifically, not that they necessarily agreed with the ideas, but for their interest, comments and time, which were much appreciated: John Bazlinton, Nigel Chamberlain and Graeme Robins; James Pringle, Philip Wintle and Alan Gordon; Anthony Werner of Shepheard-Walwyn; Kate Deaud for word-processing and Dominic Stoppani for the cover. And the many other people, family, friends and others, who showed interest and sometimes gave specific help.

Contents

Guide to key points

1

FREE LUNCHES

(Are you getting them?)

The Restaurant

Deep down in folk memory, there lingers for most people
the thought that they should somehow be entitled to Free Lunches.
From time to time they pass the Free Lunch Restaurant and this stirs hope,
and they dream about Free Lunches for a while.
The Free Lunch Restaurant has been in business ever since society began and its
supplies, both in originality and variety are mouth-wateringly delicious.

People regard Free Lunches in a variety of ways.

Despite the common saying that: 'There is no such thing as a free lunch',
many of the diners at the Free Lunch Restaurant rarely eat anywhere else.

Some of the people who pass by can see that the place is packed and they glimpse the
sumptuous fare, but they never think that they too might enjoy Free Lunches.
It is beyond their understanding how this could be,
even if it is not beyond their dreams.

Others are loitering by the door
expectant that it will soon be their turn to choose from the menu.
These people have hopes about Free Lunches,
but disappointment dawns as they realise that no table will be laid for them.

Some people, at very busy times, get a table near the door and start to eat
but their Free Lunch makes them sick and they have to leave in a hurry.

Many of those who do enjoy a modest meal are somewhat puzzled.
They seem to have misunderstood something about their particular Free Lunch.

The lunch has cost them dearly.

The Alaskan Free Lunch

IN THE YEAR 2000 every citizen in the state of Alaska received a personal payment equivalent to £1400 so that a family of four received about £5600. Since 1982, growing annual payments have been possible because it had been decided that some of the newly found oil wealth must be given directly to citizens rather than taken solely by the state. The profit from an earlier oil bonanza had disappeared in state-run schemes and there was a fear that this would happen again unless steps were taken to safeguard the wealth for current and future generations of Alaskan citizens. There are no strings attached to the personal payment, people can do exactly what they want with the money, and thus every Alaskan is enjoying a genuine Free Lunch. Check the website of the Alaskan Permanent Fund! (Appendix C). In contrast, in the parallel case of the United Kingdom, which developed its oilfields at the same time, no such citizen-oriented scheme has ever been set up. All the wealth has been poured into government coffers and there is no fund accumulating for the future benefit of UK citizens as there is for Alaskans when the oil runs out.

The experience of the ignorant, the disappointed and the puzzled, of The Restaurant allegory, gives credence to the modern proverb *'There is no such thing as a free lunch'*. But the folk memory surfaces from time to time and refreshes itself, with the example of Alaska for instance. By the time you have finished reading this book you will have become more aware of a particular variety of Free Lunches that are being 'served' in our society, and also how you fit into that scenario. You may be enjoying these Free Lunches yourself (or think you are), but certainly you will be contributing to Free Lunches for others. You will also discover that it is quite possible to provide Free Lunches for everyone.

An example of a Free Lunch is that associated with land value. This can be looked at quite separately from the value of any house or building on it. It is the *value of the land* that actually produces the huge jumps in property values that make the headlines. The selling price of a 'house' can gain 20% in a year but with building costs only rising at about 3%, the main increase in value of an unimproved house is due to the rising value of the land. But why has the plot of land underlying a building in an expensive part of London, such as Mayfair, such a high value? It is the result of the successful society that has grown up around it. And what defines a successful society? It is where the phones and electricity work, the rubbish is collected, the streets are safe; the banks are open and businesses run; the media is uncensored and children are learning; law is respected and there is a democratic procedure for changing laws. Clearly all the people who live and work nearby, and out into the rest of London and the South East of England, contribute to the success; be they shop assistants, taxi drivers, fashion designers, bankers, bakers, or property developers. All, together, make London thrive and this is reflected in the high cost of land generally and the very high cost of Mayfair land. Most of them will have nothing to do with the particular plot of land in Mayfair. However, whether they have a high powered or a humble job, they will all be doing a little to make the whole of the South East of England economically successful, and culturally and socially desirable.

The popular adage has it that 'the three most important factors determining property values are: 'location, location, location!' The house is actually of secondary importance in terms of value, it can be modified or re-built, if sub-standard, but it is the land location that is of prime concern. Within the total asking price, land has a separate value that is rarely acknowledged. London is a profitable place to live and work and for the many facilities available. The Mayfair location in particular is considered especially desirable, and its high price reflects the demand. But notice that although everyone is contributing to the success, it is only freeholders and landowners who gain the Free Lunch from the underlying land values that come directly from that success. If you are a nurse, teacher, or shop assistant, for example, however vital you are to people's health or the education of the rising generation, if you can only afford to rent a flat, there is no land value Free Lunch for you. If the only flat you can afford is some distance from your workplace you will also be incurring high travel costs.

Articles in the media about property values tell of road improvements such as a bypass that can bring a 10-15% rise in the price of local houses. This is a good example of a Free Lunch for a few freeholders, paid for by everyone nationwide through their taxes. Also, within the catchment area of a good school, it has been noted that the value of an average house can increase by £10,000, and sometimes much more. Parents who are ambitious for their children, choose to live there, bid up 'house' prices (although actually, it is only the underlying land prices that are rising so fast). The hard work and success of the staff at these schools has created a particular Free Lunch to all the freeholders of these areas, most of whom would have had no connection with the school. Ironically, these successful teachers who create the high demand for the school which forces up house prices in the area, may mean they are unable to afford one themselves!

Some of the Free Lunches to be examined are based on gifts of nature which existed unused before human society began; apart from land, these Free Lunches might include such things as: oil, gas, coal, other minerals, radio waves, water and tidal currents. Other types of Free Lunch only exist because a society exists and creates a demand for them: like rights of way over roads and paths, credit in the banking system and such things as aircraft landing time slots. The benefits that flow from this great and growing variety of resources are here named Free Lunches. They improve life and as there is high demand for them, they are usually given a monetary value. Resources of land or coal, for instance, were there for the taking, and those who got there first and cleared the forest for cultivation or worked the seams, gained the Free Lunch value for themselves.

Warm glow or despair?

The news that house prices are rising by 20% per annum can bring different reactions:

- A sense of wellbeing for homeowners
- A sense of hopelessness for those wanting their first dwelling.
  They may have to give up trying; or move a hundred miles.

Most people spend a large part of their waking hours earning as an employee and their pay is simply a compensation for the time they have given to attending someone else's venture. Employee perks such as paid holidays and pension rights are very welcome but are merely compensation for the loss of freedom and personal choice. Profits in most businesses are usually generated from the combined creativity of all employees, although some businesses largely exist to gather the extra profits flowing from Free Lunches.

Many people hope to win the top prize in the National Lottery which is in effect a massive Free Lunch. The huge odds against such an event do not deter millions in the futile pursuit of their dream. For the vast majority, a big win is only ever a fantasy, and the expense of the habit curtails choice of spending elsewhere, without any compensating benefit apart perhaps from minor wins. But the popularity of such schemes speaks volumes for the expectation that Free Lunches of some sort might just be possible. One of the attractions of partaking in the Lottery is that a certain amount of the proceeds goes to charities and cultural causes which are certainly enjoying Free Lunches. There are principles on which Lotteries depend that show very clearly what normally happens to Free Lunches, of which more later.

Many of us have been given free shares when a 'mutual' building society has become a bank. People earned the basic quota of free shares merely through having been a member of the building society, regardless of their balance size. This idea has a strong parallel with the principle that all citizens should have Free Lunch rights merely through being a citizen. In the case of building societies the recognition of the equal status of members was necessary to secure votes for the conversion, and the incentive usually worked. But the mutual idea is not completely defunct despite the success of the conversions, which may tell more about the lack of ready capital among the members, than any particular merit of banks over 'mutuals'.

Millions of council houses have been sold to the sitting tenant at large discounts to market value. These involve the handing over of the Free Lunch in land values from state ownership to individuals and families. The new mortgage payments are probably higher than rent, but the payments do eventually end, in contrast to rent. But as the owner has to pay for repairs, there is an extra cost with acquiring this Free Lunch. An important theme of this book is increase in choice and the new owners of ex-council houses certainly have gained this. They now have rights to alter and improve their house and this is an intrinsic, non-financial benefit.

Did the privatisation sales of our national utilities like British Telecom and British Gas involve the handing out of Free Lunches? Some of these concerns were set up to supply society with products using natural resources and thus were based on the Free Lunch concept, and the Free Lunch value was taken through nationalisation into the remit of government 'on behalf of the people'. When they were sold off back into private ownership, like the council house case, they were offered at discounts to their true value and those who bought the shares gained the regular flow of dividends and for a while at least, rising share values. Those who took up the offers were getting, along with the profits and risks of share investment, some measure of a Free Lunch that everyone's taxes had partly funded through the years. Those who could not join in the sale lost out. Elsewhere, in ex-Soviet Russia for instance, privatisation was carried with the intention of benefiting every citizen. Everyone was issued a

personal stake, free, in the privatised utilities. As all had contributed to
the creation and functioning of these enterprises, so all were to benefit
at privatisation.

The Lottery Principle

Except for the Alaskan case, most of the above Free Lunches have
common features. Only a limited number of people enjoy them and
their value depends on the contributions of many other people. For
example, the National Lottery prizewinners, and the good causes, gain
out of all proportion to any contribution they made individually; their
gains are entirely due to the complete loss of ticket money by the
losers. The Lottery is an obvious refutation of the phrase: 'There is no
such thing as a free lunch'. The fundamentals of lotteries are helpful to
this study.

The history of wealth distribution within societies shows
similarities to the way lotteries work. The underlying tendency could
be named the 'Lottery Principle', defined as the process in society
whereby: *'The poor create the rich'*. This statement attempts to
encapsulate how wealth moves in all societies. It is a purpose of this
book to show how, by allowing the richer to capture nature's and
society's, valuable Free Lunches, this further enriches them. Also, to
show how the process imposes high costs on all and in doing so,
maintains the poor in their poverty. Much government and charitable
action arises to combat the working of the Lottery Principle but it too
often deals with symptoms and not causes. The aim of this book is to
show how the root of the problem could be tackled so that the grip of
the Lottery Principle might be loosened. In doing this, a theme is
promoted that shows how individuals could be more creative, enjoy
more choice and retain more fruit of their own success.

THE LOTTERY PRINCIPLE:
'The poor create the rich'

But what does 'poverty' mean. Who are the 'poor'? For some
people poverty endures through generations and clearly, they never
seem to be in a 'winning team'. But even in the ranks of those of us
who do appear to be managing financially, many are a mere 'two pay
days away from bankruptcy'. Despite the ability to survive somewhat
precariously for years like this, by such definitions many people might
be described as poor. Many household budgets depend upon a job in a

precarious industry. Some find that they are obliged to work seven days a week, or work unsocial hours to pay their way, and families can suffer as parents absent themselves from home at these times. The book will examine aspects of how our society operates and contrast these with fairer ways of doing things. In so doing, the reader's understanding of what poverty is may be modified.

One area will involve the matter of house purchase. People have to commit a large part of their earnings over a long period to it, rather than, for instance, use spare cash to start a small business. Those who cannot manage to start buying a house, will have to pay high rent for their whole lifetime. They never gain the security of a place of their own, and do not gain for themselves any of the benefits that the Free Lunch in land values brings. Despite hundreds of thousands of empty homes, homelessness has not been abolished and one household in four needs to have their housing costs subsidised, a transaction which helps to maintain the landlord's Free Lunch derived from land value. That some workers vital to our health and education services are becoming unable to afford to rent or buy even the cheapest of accommodation in some areas, must be having a negative effect on the well-being of our society. At the same time land availability is so highly restricted that some new houses are built on sites which result in appalling amenity, such as within the very shadow of gargantuan elevated motorways or on land prone to flooding. Others are built at the edges of towns in dense developments that sweep like tidal waves into the adjoining countryside and give rise to the NIMBY (Not In My Back Yard) tendencies that increasingly oppose them. Everywhere homes are being built ever-closer together resulting in the general debasement of the urban environment, with increased air pollution, more traffic and neighbour problems due to crowded living. The planning system which allocates housing land, protects those people already favoured environmentally, who are often enjoying a good Free Lunch in their property value, at the expense of the rest. The Lottery Principle is given an added, non-financial twist in that *'the environmentally poor support the environmentally rich'*. Meanwhile the countryside is left largely empty whilst some farmers desperately need alternative income.

'The market' is now recognized as a vital key in supplying society's needs efficiently. But the above outcomes in the housing market indicate that a monopoly is at work. Monopolies arise when there is a limited supply of a product that is in great demand, and consequently prices are forced higher. We connect the monopoly idea with one or a few powerful firms that manage to corner the market in important products, increase their prices and take high profits. The government tackles commercial monopolies so that we do not have to pay unnecessarily high prices for essential goods. However, when it comes to the equally important need to have somewhere to live, there is no similar device to moderate the monopolistic character of the land and the housing market. High demand acting on a limited supply of houses and land, causes huge price increases, usually far in excess of general inflation.

The economy works with a mind of its own as business booms for a while. Then just when we started to believe what our current Chancellor of the Exchequer was telling us about 'conquering' economic volatility, a recession came round again to surprise us, and jobs disappear. Especially at these times do those who have few resources become burdensome to others. State expenses keep climbing in relatively good economic times, which means they will become uncomfortably large in times of economic recession and deliver even bigger burdens to future generations. Governments take the risk, if they raise taxes openly, of being voted out of office, so they increasingly devise ever more stealthy taxation. This gives rise to the business of 'tax planning' which involves expensive advice from creative people for their work, which inevitably loads a greater burden on those who have no scope for such planning to reduce their own tax bill.

With increasingly global markets, government revenues are endangered as companies find they have to use cheaper labour in developing countries, or lose competitive advantage. How can the individual citizen and the local small business compete fairly in a contest where the field is dominated with national and global players, and where national wealth arising from Free Lunch value is unevenly spread? Hierarchies of many sorts govern parts of our lives, individuals often feel powerless and human relationships suffer.

Serena and Venus Williams, David Beckham

Whereas war is an attempt to dominate at any cost, games are an attempt to excel under strict guidelines. The aim is to win through fair play, according to meticulously developed rules as overseen by an umpire or referee, and hopefully without match-fixing. Each player or team gives their best, having prepared through training. The result should be as much as possible due to skill, and as little as possible due to bias, chance and cheating. Under the rules in tennis for example, using such devices as the division of the match into sets and games, timed pauses, changes of end, and much incremental scoring, the odds are smoothed out, so that fairness reigns and skill predominates. If a player is serving into the sun, the disadvantage reverses as ends are changed; racquets must comply with a standard pattern. Imagine if Serena Williams was on a winning streak and her sister Venus was battling at the other end against the glare of a low sun, and the umpire did not allow the normal change of ends to take place!

In team games an injured player can be replaced by a fit one, and rest breaks are taken equally by all. Millions champion their favourite team or player and take it for granted that all players and teams have the same opportunity of displaying their skill. But imagine a game of football being played where after every goal that David Beckham scored, the goalposts he was aiming between were moved apart by one metre! These bizarre suggestions demonstrate how within the game, justice reigns to an unusual extent compared with everyday life, where the reality is of hard struggles against heavy odds; where there seems to be no 'half-time' and where many seem often to be 'playing uphill with the sun in their eyes'. Life is in great contrast to the 'level playing field' of the game. That this last metaphor is borrowed for use in other contexts illustrates how game playing is a benchmark for the sense of fair play. The equal treatment that players receive in a game, the essence of its fairness, is often absent in the real world. Although many of us are poor, most of the rest of us manage to survive economically, but an unfavourable shift in the economic wind may easily disrupt our lives.

Centuries of material progress and much enlightened reform have not shifted disparities of opportunity and wealth in our society. We have not found a way to achieve a fundamental fairness for all, where everyone would survive without undue burden, none would be overwhelmed, but where those who were capable and determined would achieve high rewards. Fairness as a foundational principle has little impact in the way we run things.

How is it that we slip so easily between the game culture and our normal lives, operate so differently in each, and yet rarely comment on the contrast between the two? The unfairness experienced in the daily lives of many people is far removed from any game worthy of the name. Despite much socio-political experimentation, state welfare provision for millions is as necessary now as it ever was. Is sport so popular because it provides an idealistic relief from the difficult background of daily life? Why do we put up with these imbalances which if they arose in a game would end play in minutes?

There are those who campaign for greater fairness, and there are those who challenge such ideas as being incompatible with the freedom of others. But within these pages the hope is to show that there are ways of organizing things which would keep the important issues of justice and freedom in harmony, so that ordinary life for all of us, whatever our capabilities, could become very much fairer, more like a game, and as enjoyable.

2

MOSES' BIG IDEA

(An ancient antidote to the Lottery Principle)

This chapter introduces an ancient philosophical basis and model for a fair society that recognized basic human economic rights for all. It is not an essential part of the book's argument but it reinforces the reasoning in the chapters that follow and is referred to in them. The principles, practical examples and historical references are helpful for understanding the themes of the whole book. However the reader who would rather not take this historical diversion at this point should read sub-section E of this chapter before proceeding to Chapter 3, *The Citizens Royalty.*

A. FAIRNESS: The economy as a game

IN EVERY SPORT AND GAME, to competitive people, winning is everything, but for the game to take place at all, rules are essential. Umpires' decisions and cheating are aspects of games that relate directly to the rules, whether it is the umpire's interpretation of them or the cheat's avoidance of them. Fair play, which can only take place when rules are respected, makes for a good game. Moses, who to this day is honoured by Jews, Christians and Muslims was the instigator of a society that ran for some hundreds of years following a system that has close parallels with game-playing. Although in Moses' time that society was made possible through conquest, for us the principles of it can be adopted by democratic consent.

Freedom, hope and compassion are elusive, given the constraints of political and economic reality, but 3000 years ago the pastoral society we shall be examining had a framework of laws to foster just such qualities. Judged by the standards of any age the Mosaic ideas show the mind of an extraordinarily enlightened political scientist and economist. The economy was designed to be run with the fairness characterising a game, with all citizens as active players who started each 'round' with resources for self-support - their own 'Free Lunch'. They were to be *independent and interdependent rather than subservient.* They were to be free and were empowered to be economically creative by having their own land. Politics and economics were thoroughly intertwined for everyone. The provision of sustenance and housing were their own responsibility. If the going got too tough for some, the system was realistic enough to cope with failure by the temporary expedient of dependency on others. However the timings for these periods were to be controlled as strictly as a referee with a stopwatch in a game, and the poor would return to their own resources in due course. The concept of mercy is integral to the Mosaic system. For instance, as will be seen later, debt forgiveness and weekly rest day incorporate both compassion and hope. Our modern system throws the poor onto whatever 'mercy' individuals might show them, or onto the state provision paid for through 'involuntary charity' (taxation) and involves begrudged income top-ups but with no hope of resources to set the poor up again.

The Mosaic system was a counter to the Lottery Principle that societies are usually operating under. There were real advantages for those who were successful and ambitious, since some disparities of wealth were not permanently eliminated. Winning was not banned or penalised, it was encouraged; and indeed the poor would depend on the success of others during their own difficult times, but extreme and unremitting poverty was constantly guarded against. Both *human empowerment* and *environmental sustainability* were fostered, through the right to permanent long term ownership. Since the allocated natural land resources were to be the source of survival and wealth for following generations in the same family, the current generation had a personal vested interest in maintaining and nurturing them. They were also protected against exploitation from outsiders, who were not permitted to buy them up, exploit them and depart.

The realities of modern economic life, as experienced by many people are more like a conflict, or drudgery, than a fair contest. A large bureaucracy is needed as governments tackle symptoms, redressing the worst economic disadvantages suffered by the poorest; but the measures are generally late, usually feeble, can sometimes fail to achieve much and may aggravate matters. Some people get locked into poverty. Fraud generates more expense to fight it. Although technology has transformed life and work, there are great disparities of of asset ownership, enduring welfare needs and a huge tax burden. The principles behind Moses' arrangements should not be dismissed as irrelevant outside the original pastoral society. Moses' system was without a central political authority, apart from management of the legal system. His system allowed *creativity* to flourish within a simple set of guidelines and included *relaxation and celebration* as important features. Life was for enjoying and not to be all toil.

Key principle or pious platitude?

One phrase that encapsulates the theme of Moses' system is: *love your neighbour as yourself*, (Refs. Appendix C). The laws that relate to inter-personal relationships and dealings are all rooted in it. The principle is used today as little more than a platitude and as such implies that it only applies to idealists, such as legendary charity workers. However the genius of the phrase is that it was intended to be the summary, or guideline, for many practical laws and regulations. It defines the level of altruism by reference to everyone's everyday personal experience and feelings. It accepts as normal that people will look after themselves and indeed uses this self-centred reference point as the gauge of acceptable treatment towards others. It covers more than a strictly individualistic viewpoint than the point of reference 'yourself' because this word would inevitably include for a parent, for instance, their own children and grandchildren. But the balance of: concern for 'me and mine' against that for 'neighbour and theirs', was to set the paradigm for all the Judaistic laws and regulations.

Thus the laws give structure so that the hoped for mutuality of feelings could affect practical everyday action. This includes a wide range of behaviour all the way from strict interpretation of the law in the manner of 'you scratch my back and I'll scratch yours' to heroic selflessness ('pure' altruism), beyond any specific regulation. The phrase is also a foundational principle for all new law, for all those new departures and interpretations of the law that were necessary as society develops. The laws and regulations show that there were practical issues to be taken account of, which impact on rights and duties for every citizen in society. It was so much more than a platitude to be followed by the pious believer on a good day,

Rights and responsibilities

Founders of other world religions said similar things to Moses. The founder of Islam, Mohammed, said: 'No one of you is a true believer until he desires for his brother that which he desires for himself'; and

Baha'ullah similarly: 'blessed is he who preferreth his brother before himself'. However the ideas to be examined should not be seen as religious in a narrow sense. The Mosaic regulations that defined religious ceremonial observance or crime and punishment are not of concern to this book. What will be of concern are civil matters where the moral imperative of *'love your neighbour as yourself'* was worked out in practical economic, financial and political terms. The power of this foundational idea was behind specific laws concerning such things as land ownership, business and employment, welfare provision, communal time management, health and safety, and so on. The laws gave everyone the same access to the resources of the earth (land rights), and were fundamental to the freedom of the whole society and not a gimmick. *'Love your neighbour as yourself'* was the ideology underpinning the provision of 'something for everyone' and the laws spelt out rights and responsibilities to ensure this. This would prevent the resources from drifting into limited hands with large scale poverty establishing itself, which is what usually happens in a society under the Lottery Principle. The law was to maintain a fundamental economic fairness in society that for us, by comparison, is shallow or non-existent.

Walls and latrines, wooden spoons and blood clotting
The economic and political principles behind Moses' laws from a modern worldview will be examined shortly. Moses' system was rooted in the common human condition as he, and we also, know it. Some specific regulations about matters other than economics, were intensely practical and relevant for everyone, then and now, and some contain extraordinary insights.

One of the Mosaic regulations covered the building of a wall around the accessible flat roof of the houses of those times. Anyone even now 3000 years later, can see the sense in this rule and benefit from it. We have no dispute with Moses' advice concerning this safety regulation, it demonstrates the high value placed on human life. The house owner was to provide the wall to protect, for example, a neighbour's wandering child, who might be in danger of falling off. This is a practical application of *'love your neighbour as yourself'*, and demonstrates how such a guideline can be understood as reasonable by any person of good will whether they have a religious belief or none. No piety it required of the builder or owner to carry out such a precaution; humanitarian concern in any society ensures that such safety precautions are made law. Today we have precisely that type of building regulation as a sensible precaution against injury or death and many, many more, as befits the complex technology that has developed since Moses' day.

There were simple regulations about latrines that are elementary to the design of some sewage systems even today (taking sewage away from living areas and burying it).

One regulation stipulated that the metal cooking implements used by a household that had been affected by a contagious disease were to be put in the fire to purify them; earthenware was to be put beyond use by smashing it; but wooden implements were merely to be washed with water. This was not an economy measure since even a house was to be destroyed in some cases. In the last decade it has been discovered that hardwood has properties that destroy bacteria, thus somehow, 3000 years before modern science, Moses understood that wooden implements were naturally hygienic, but that metal ones were not.

Another insight concerns the practise of male circumcision on the eighth day. Whatever the purpose of this practice, the significance of the eighth day has only been known scientifically within recent times. That is the day when the clotting capacity of human blood rises to a peak following birth and thereafter declines!

These examples should lead us to examine carefully the possibility of timeless principles behind the economic laws and the socio-political norms given by Moses. These are replete with hope and values that resonate with our desire for a fair society, yet they acknowledge the practicalities of the real world. Of 'The Ten' commandments of Moses, numbers one to three fit into a category that can be described as about human-to-God relationships (love God with all your mind, heart and strength); and numbers four to ten into a second category of human-to-human relationships, (love your neighbour as yourself). This book is only concerned with some of the second category. The safety wall was an aspect of number six which was concerned with the taking of human life. Number eight: 'You shall not steal' covered the land laws that stipulated that the poor must have their family land returned at the fifty year Jubilee occasion.

'Love your neighbour as yourself' – even in economics?
Everyone wants the life of good relationships, prosperity and security. In a few phrases Moses is recorded as telling of the good outcomes the people would enjoy whether in city and country; the promising families they would rear; the profitable farming ventures they would

create; and of their elevated international role. Safe travel was assured, international financial power was to be theirs and they would not succumb to warlike neighbours. With security, health, and prosperity those times were to be characterised by 'shalom': well-being, peace, fairness, compassion and justice. The boldness of the statements about these benefits, if they were propounded at a modern election, would probably be looked at quite cynically by sophisticated modern electorates.

But Moses' 'manifesto' was not a declaration in the manner of a modern politician, who would promise to change things for the better, without costing the majority much. In his system there were no politicians or central regime. Rather, Moses was saying that as long as everyone respected everyone else's rights, good results for all would follow. Moses, and later on Joshua, Deborah and Samuel would exhort the people to expect beneficial outcomes if they would keep laws and observe regulations. These included: limited rights over a debtor's land; the granting of loans, and the cancelling of them; taking a garment in pledge, but returning it each evening; observing a national holiday one day each week; and so on. This was not a formula for a fanciful Utopia. It was a realistic way for a society to prosper as it regularly re-empowered people to realise their creative potential and gave them resources to do so and to act compassionately. *It promoted fairness and took full account of the realities of random misfortune, selfishness and variable human talent.*

Fundamental to the Mosaic view of society is the sanctity of human life – on a practical level how else would the nation endure and thrive unless this was so? *But beyond this basic preservation of life there is a continuing high view of the rights for quality of life for all,* and the basic right to land for all would ensure this. The people were not required to love neighbour *'more* than yourself' but *'as* yourself'. How would I like to be treated if I were experiencing what this other person person is now going through?', or 'Do unto others as you would have them do unto you'. This ability to hypothesise internally is possible for most people, so that such an exhortation can promote a fairness and reasonable standard of behaviour, with rights and responsibilities within any culture or society. However, laws and regulations are necessary to prevent doubt and the frustration of continually redefining what 'fair' means in every case and to prevent the selfish and strong taking advantage of the weak. The philosopher John Rawls used 'disinterested unselfishness' as a basic tool in determining fairness in society. He said that judgements about justice (welfare for the poorest and reward for the most able) should be decided by imagining ourselves to be in ignorance about our own potential with respect to everyone else. That is, forcing us to act in the extreme cases, with ourselves being either the least, or the most talented.

Moses

Slave-child, prince, celebrity, murderer, fugitive, wonderworker, military strategist and national leader, Moses became one of the world's most renowned law-givers, and was a highly original political scientist and economist. Knowing Moses' life story and his times, we would not naturally expect one of the fundamental political principles of his Law to be that ordinary people should be given rights to basic resources and be trusted with their own destiny. This is one measure of Moses' genius. His dates are uncertain and estimates of his birth range from 1500BC to 1200BC.

The 12 tribes that were descended from the children of Jacob had spent centuries in Egypt, and as a large and distinct ethnic group were perceived to be a threat to the host country. Thus did the Hebrews became exploited to provide the menial labour for the Egyptian regime, a slavery-based economic system running purely on Lottery Principle lines. The current Pharoah was advocating a policy of male infanticide with female babies being allowed to survive, presumably for the purpose of providing the breeding stock for new slaves to keep the labour force up to strength. Actually the pro-life principles of the Hebrew midwives were strong enough to engage in civil disobedience and they refused to follow the palace line.

There is an intriguing story in the book of Exodus about how Moses survived to be brought up as a prince. When he became adult, aware of his true heritage as one of the oppressed, he saw an Egyptian beating a Hebrew slave and murdered the man. The news got out and Moses' had to escape.

He settled in a nearby country, married Zipporah and raised a family. After a long time he moved back to Egypt and became the man who led the Hebrews out of Egypt and slavery. Curiously for someone so successful in this role he appears to have suffered some kind of speech-block, which meant that he always needed someone else to speak for him at crucial times.

Thus, given this ignorance, since I might be poor I would not load the odds against them and in favour of the rich. But I would have to not only 'play for safety' just in case I found myself at the bottom of the heap, but also recognise the need to reward success because I might be successful myself one day. These ideas of fair play have a strong resonance with the Mosaic principles as encapsulated in: *'love your neighbour as yourself'*.

Under these ideals, people could deal with each other from a

secure personal base, which is a necessary element to good relationships. To allow no rights, but to expect responsible action encourages
dictatorial power and promotes slavery. A strongly hierarchical society or organization can debase relationships, since many of these will
carry a strong superior/inferior aspect that precludes the robust
equality that is essential to meaningful and successful human
interaction. The Mosaic way fostered good relationships through the
dynamic of powerful networks across and between the families, the
only hierarchical arrangements being within families. With their
material security based largely in the asset base of their own family
land, people could relate as equals.

B. TIMING : Short and Long Term Rights

The Free Lunch in the pastoral society: Land

At every fiftieth year, the Jubilee, everyone was to return to 'family
property' and to 'family' and this links two fundamental provisions,
the material and the social, at the heart of Moses' wealth system.
Firstly, every family was to grow their own food through working
their land and provide their own accommodation on it; and secondly
they would support, and be supported by, the network of people that
consisted of their family, clan, tribe and nation. Because these all
owned land too, they would be empowered to co-operate, building
their own lives and hopefully helping the poor. Land was thus the
basis of essentials for survival: a site for family housing and fields for
food, and also the base for additional prosperity and entrepreneurial
development. Any success beyond mere survival would be very much
dependent on the skill within the family and would be variable
between families.

We hold our wealth in a more individualistic manner whereby
usually one or two people hold the generation's wealth with no
particular view of the very long term family interest. A family trust
might be formed, but these are largely for the purpose of safeguarding
long term wealth beyond the reach of the state revenue system. This
achieves some wealth conservation for the richer families of our
society but in the Mosaic system the family tenure system did this for
every family. Also, for the ambitious and successful there was the
opportunity to own other houses, away from those on their family
land, in most of the walled towns, in perpetuity, beyond the 'Jubilee
return'. These could be bought and sold on an open market basis. This

gave the choice of a further homes, but the system ensured that all owned at least one.

Moses' system categorised the tribes into two groups, that is, the Levites and the rest. The Levites carried out religious and some legal functions and were the only 'central' authority. They had no land except the limited pasture around their towns. Their income was a tax or tithe (10%) on the increase of all produce of all the other tribes. At a census just prior to the conquest they had accounted for less than 4% of the population. Thus, at that time, about half the tithe would have provided for them and half for their various religious, charitable and judicial duties. Foreigners still remaining in the land or settling later did not have the same statutory rights to land in perpetuity, or rights to release from a term of slavery, but they were not restricted from becoming wealthy and they could employ Israelite slaves. It was expected that foreigners would be given employment, and they were not to be treated harshly or as enemies.

'Planning Policy'

Moses, by allotting the land piecemeal to families over the entire country, was operating a 'planning policy' based on even-handed dispersal. This suited the pastoral nature of the society and the overall defence of the nation as all corners of the land would be occupied and owned by specific families. *The policy had political implications, in that no one family could build up a power base flowing from the economic wealth residing in especially large land holdings.* Joshua who oversaw the land allocation after the conquest, did not create for himself, as military leader, a special bounty in a generous landholding which could have become a base for political ambitions of his family. This was rare restraint. The centuries that followed without the need for a monarch are a witness to the wisdom of the arrangements.

Time Cycles

The division of the land according to families, clans and tribes rather than individuals was an important feature in ensuring that all had a stake together. The performance of the family group and the medium term retention of their land thereby depended on the sum of the abilities of the group, all of whom had an interest in the well-being of their land, which would have helped to ensure a viable economic unit. However, despite the initial fairness, the ownership of resources drifted temporarily, through the variable capabilities of the families, and life's normal vagaries, towards the more successful. The cyclical adjustments ensured that, through debt cancellation, employment release and land restoration, everyone was re-empowered, thus preventing the development of a permanent underclass and a wealthy elite. Land could not be sold permanently and there were strict rules about prices for land sold, which were related only to the number of harvests until the Jubilee year. Between times, free economic activity had its way and the capable thrived. Thus Moses achieved a realistic balance, over time, between market freedoms, the prevention of destitution for the unsuccessful, the successful creativity of the more able, and the need to keep the land in good heart.

Rests and celebration

The weekly rest for one day ran through the entire Jubilee, 50 year cycle.
The yearly break occurred in the seventh year when debts which had built up in the preceding six years were to be cancelled; and when people who had had to enter employment were to be released from it.
Heavy sowing and judicious storage as the six year work-cycle drew to a close, would have built up supplies to ensure survival during the cropping-break of year seven.

The fiftieth (Jubilee) year, was an extra rest year, when the poor were to have their family land restored, enabling them to be self-reliant again.

Rest years were to be celebratory as people left their employment, their debts vanished and they regained their family land.

The fiftieth (Jubilee) year proclamation 'Freedom!' or 'Liberty!', shows how vital was the possession of land in those times. For us today, these words imply release from prison or from the rule of a harsh regime, that is, the mere absence of unwelcome restraint - a somewhat limited notion. But when Israelite families heard this celebratory announcement they would have been envisioned with the return to their own land and self-reliance once again - such was their deep and positive understanding of 'Freedom!'

One purpose of the marker day or year at the end of each time cycle, whether seven day, seven yearly or fifty yearly, was that all were to experience the benefit of the luxury of rest at the same time. They would be reminded that times had been so different for their forebears in the unrelenting slavery of Egypt. The enjoyment of the periodic respite from work would lead to an appreciation of the remarkable freedoms and the inherent fairness of Moses' system.

Inevitably through the six years of the lesser cycles and through each forty nine years of the greater ones, wealth would tend to become more concentrated within certain families. But the periodic adjustments at seventh and fiftieth years redressed the inequalities. Modern governments attempt wealth readjustments and redistribution using a year-on-year approach through taxation, but it fails to shift deep rooted poverty because it fails to make a permanent long term economic difference for the poor that the possession of land did in Moses' system. Also, rather than allow the economy to burst into life and then die down, a feature of modern times is to try and tame the economy in the boom and frantically revive it in the bust. In Mosaic terms modern business cycles would be described as running to a rhythm of 'work/rest/work/rest', which is a more positive way to describe them than: 'boom/bust/boom/bust'.

The system nurtured the creativity of all, even of those who had slipped back over time into poverty. Employment by other people, usually the highest aspiration of the modern citizen, was only a useful stop-gap measure for the poor who were perhaps in debt, until they could be free to work entirely for themselves again, or as they eventually went back to their own land.

Egalitarianism as currently understood involves the ideal of equal rights and opportunities for all, as a *constant feature*. Moses' system allowed the successful to progress but ensured that certain minimum rights and realisable opportunities protected the poor. Thus the system allowed rights, responsibilities and opportunities to become *increasingly unbalanced* as the six years passed but every seventh (and fiftieth) year the poor were to be favoured. Moses, with realism and ingenuity, set marker years triggering *alternating time periods of 'unequal' rights and opportunities,* in order to build a strong and fair society which grew and maintained fairness with freedom for as long as the rules were observed.

Moses' cyclical system was to run in a primitive pastoral economy and we can only surmise as to what agricultural and ecological benefits, if any, every seventh year and fiftieth year land-rests might achieve; apart from the psychological and therapeutic effects for the people. The resting of the land by lying fallow may be part of the answer but this could have been achieved in any year on a rotation basis. Are there benefits in leaving vast areas of land fallow at the same time? Other reasons for the particular length of the cycles could include the varying activity within the normal human life span and in inter-generational relationship patterns.

Judges, Kings & Prophets

Joshua, Moses' assistant, was a Judge at the time of the conquest of the land. Possibly four centuries ensued until the last Judge, Samuel, was prevailed upon to usher in the monarchy. The Judges were ad-hoc leaders who rose to prominence through their legal expertise and leadership skills. Those named are often related to times of crisis when the people were suffering threats of invasion. A Judge would become a focus for a national movement which repelled the invaders and restored respect for the Law. The Biblical books of Judges and Ruth record these times. The subsequent change to the monarchy superimposed an hierarchical political system and it is clear from the record that respect and even knowledge of the Mosaic laws was very much reduced.

For just over a century during the reign of the first three kings: Saul, David and Solomon, the nation remained united and powerful, but at Solomon's death the northern part of the kingdom broke away. Over the next four centuries exile followed the invasion of both parts, as other nations from north and south used Israel as a bridge or a buffer between Africa and Asia in their own empire building strategies. See the books of Samuel, Kings and Chronicles.

Prophets who operated throughout the above periods were often from unexpected backgrounds. Their messages almost always had the plight of the poor and disadvantaged as important elements, as the rules of the national game reverted from the Free Lunch ideals of Moses to the Lottery Principle of standard human society. They campaigned for closer observance of the spirit of the Law to benefit all the people and were not afraid to name names at the highest level of society.

The benefits of the breaks within the cycles were, firstly, that the recreational and re-establishing needs of the temporarily disadvantaged were considered to be a priority over further material gains for the more successful. The timetabling of these rests on a national basis made them easily enforceable. Whilst the maximising of individual choice as to the timing of a rest period might seem desirable, it would be impossible to monitor that everyone was receiving their rights of rest without the bureaucratic intrusion that similar modern legislation leads to.

The modern viewpoint is to press for the freedom of businesses to trade at all times. Thus to some of us it might seem somewhat curious, not to say risky, to break the flow of such a simple subsistence economy with the one year stop in planting and harvest. If an employee ('slave') was to be released in year seven and there had been no rest year, it would have meant that they would have needed to work their employee's fields in that final year as well as preparing their own. The rest year gave them a break to re-establish themselves.

A second benefit from a break is the possibility that the economy might have been invigorated *because* of break. Only sowing and planting were specifically prohibited. Animals had to be attended to; land might be cleared; and manufacture and construction involving crafts, implements, textiles, buildings, wells, roads, vehicles, tools, could be carried out as people invested in capital works.

These specific cycles of days and years ensured that life was reasonably sustainable by all. The breaks could give life a dynamic which would be similar to game playing.

C. RESPONSE TO ADVERSITY: Welfare

Charity and 'help yourself'

The first call for welfare provision for the poor, when the working of their own land failed to provide enough, was at the door of their better off relatives and neighbours, who were themselves to observe the needs of others and respond personally.

Free food for the taking of it from standing crops (an actual free lunch!), enabled people to travel without the burden of carrying food and gave the advantage of eating fresh produce. Travellers would not have to delay on their journey to seek out the owner of a crop in order buy food. This implies trust that they would not exceed the reasonable provision of handfuls of food, and use a basket, which was stealing. Whereas the other welfare regulations needed personal agreement between the participants on a case by case basis, this one relied on the honourable behaviour of travellers when the owner was not around. It is an aspect of the Free Lunch for anyone, albeit restricted to occasional handfuls of food to stave off hunger. It was a limited impersonal right to the produce of another in the course of normal activity.

Another 'help yourself' welfare, gleaning, was also an aspect of the Free Lunch but restricted to the poor. The farmer would restrain the thoroughness of the harvesting, leaving crops standing after harvest at field edges, odd uncollected sheaves, unbeaten olives or overlooked grapes. It was the right of the poor to go and harvest for themselves from these remnants. This would count as their own crop, to be gathered, transported and processed by them, thus involving them in work for their own welfare provision. But the system would have involved decisions by the farmers about how assiduous was to be their own harvesting. Certain things were defined, no second beating of olive trees, but how vigorous would the first beating be? And how wide a margin of crop would be left around the edges of fields for the poor? Assessment would have to be made about the farmer's own family needs, then the needs of the poor. How many poor were there at that time? What was the extent of their poverty? Also what was the general level of the harvest and how generous would other farmers be? If little was left for the gleaners, but later on, due to destitution, a gift or loan of food was needed, it would have been more sensible for farmers to be generous at gleaning time. If a wider margin had been left around the field edges for the poor the farmer would have saved their own family labour, in reaping, thrashing, winnowing, transport, etc. The arrangement might be affected by the proximity of the debt forgiveness year. To harvest a crop fully oneself, and then be obliged to make a loan of some of that crop only to have it shortly wiped out at debt-forgiveness time, suggests that it was better to allow a wide margin around the field for the poor to glean for themselves at harvest. With the variability of response among local farmers to different poor families there might be local political tensions, in the absence of general open-hearted generosity.

Hopefully the first line of care of the poor would be local and personal, with help coming from wider family or clan. The tenth part of the crop, the tithe, was principally intended for the tribe of the Levites. The handing over of the tithe was to be a celebration involving feasting and drinking, with the usual reminder not to neglect the poor, the alien, the widow and the fatherless. Tithes were to be taken in different years to different places, either to the centre of worship, or to the local towns, thus ensuring an evenly spread supply of stored food which would be to hand in emergency. The Levites did have their own pasture land and thus with ten percent of the national produce from the other eleven tribes they would have had spare for the the general relief of the nation. The people were exhorted to treat the poor with great compassion rather than oppress them through the power that can come through the possession of wealth. Although regulations provided a basic minimum level of support through land, employment, loans, gleaning and so on, good personal relationships between rich and poor were to encourage assistance beyond the basic rules.

Interest free loans – repayments stop at year seven
Interest on any kind of loan to fellow Israelites was banned. The wealthier person was not to take profit by charging interest for the use

of their private wealth when they made loans to the poor. To do so would be seen as the strong taking advantage of the weak and was banned as contrary to *'love your neighbour as yourself'*. It was an anti-relational action since it implies the use of power, for their own gain, from someone who should have been compassionate. It would involve, in some measure, the misuse of a monopoly power and the Mosaic system was fundamentally set against this. Just as the free picking of crops for a meal for travellers and the setting aside of crops to be gleaned by the poor showed that a part of everyone's particular success was to be available for the needs of others, so also with interest-free credit. Interest, if allowed, would mean that the rich (those with spare produce to lend) would be *made even richer by the poor* (who were desperately in need), in accordance with the Lottery Principle. But the provision for loans to the poor implies that it was not automatically expected that pure donations were the way to give welfare. A loan was to be paid back up until the next debt release year. The debt forgiveness of that seventh year was not like a modern default with the seizure of alternative assets in compensation, or the imposition of future restrictions in the manner of modern day bankruptcy. Families were to start again debt-free.

If a loan was never to last beyond six or seven years, it had served its purpose of helping a family survive up to that point and that was to be the end of the matter. The lender had no right of repayment beyond then. Loan forgiveness and the interest-free-loan principle, could be seen as reflecting that the ultimate source of the surplus wealth held by the lender had been the wider community. After all, it is impossible to create wealth in isolation, a market is needed for whatever is produced. The individual supplier is only successful as they supply an existing demand. The successful were free to gain extra wealth, but when others become poor it was their obligation to lend through compassionate concern with the possibility of no repayment. Today we try to have it all ways: interest, minimal risks, maximum profits and full repayment; but in reality we pay heavily because of the need for expensive government to look after the interests of low earners and non-earners.

Land Sale - selling the eggs but keeping the nest egg
Although every family was provided with their own land at the start, no-one was to lose it for ever, even if poverty meant that temporarily, others might cultivate it after its 'sale' raised income for the poor family. There was only one legal way to price land; it was related to

the 'cropping value' of the remaining years of the Jubilee cycle when the land reverted to the owning family at Jubilee. The deal was to be of a nature such that the price did not give advantage to one or the other. The price was not to be *above* this cropping value by charging a surplus or extra value; or to be *less* than the cropping value. No one was to take advantage of a 'community inspired' or 'location driven' rise in value of land known in classical economics as 'economic rent' or 'surplus value', which is a feature of all markets in land that are completely free (see Chapter 4). Thus, in banning 'economic rent', for the pastoral economy, Moses ensured that every family would have their 'Free Lunch' benefits from the land kept intact, and through these the means to survive and prosper independently. One generation would not be allowed to sell the family land permanently, and thus deprive the ensuing generations of their basis for self-reliant existence. This meant that there was a natural limit to the permanency and amount of welfare that a family would need since they would be self-supporting at some stage in the future, even if destitute now.

The market in land looks similar to a modern lease where property reverts to the original freeholder at a specific date, without recompense. But the difference then, compared with modern times, was that everyone, every family, was a freeholder of family land in perpetuity, whereas modern leaseholds revert to relatively few landowners rather than every family. The need to 'sell' (lease) the family land through poverty would raise income at an amount set by law, until the end of the 'lease' at Jubilee. The right to reclaim land at any time remained with the original family on a repayment related to remaining value of harvests; but at the fiftieth year the land would return to the family, without any payment at all. Whenever it was returned, the long term aim to keep the 'playing field' level for all, was achieved as the family returned to full use of their own land.

Jobs

At some stage in a slide to poverty despite all the measures of land provision, loans, eventual debt forgiveness and so on, the ultimate solution was to hire oneself as a servant or slave to someone who needed extra labour to work their own land. Employers were to realise that an Israelite servant would be good value because of the relationship. They were not to be harshly treated and if they ran off they were not to be pursued, which indicates an unusually benign form of 'slavery'. No Israelite remained employed beyond the six-year release time, unless they deliberately chose a lifetime extension at that point. Because of the possibility of loan cancellation, it follows that the successful, with their surplus wealth, would be advised to spend it and invest by improving their land or dwelling through employing the poor. They would gain permanently from this since improvements on land could never be taken from the family, unlike the lending of produce and goods. Thus works related to the land, using the labour of the poor, helped both poor and rich. You could hoard your liquid wealth; you could lend it without interest and gain goodwill by so doing (but you might lose the amount lent through later debt forgiveness); or you could spend it in wages and supplies by investing in your own future wealth through land improvements and at the same time provide work and support for the poor.

Moses' system thus incorporated incentives to investment to bring personal benefit (the entrepreneurial impulse) through the employment of others. It encouraged spare wealth to be used in ways that benefited the richer in the long term and the poor in the short term.

D. POWER: Law and Politics

Power with the people - wherever else?
Although Moses made provision for a king it appears to have been a second best as indicated by Samuel's reaction when he was pressed by the people to choose one after some centuries without. Each individual citizen's adherence to the letter and spirit of the Law was to show their religious dedication and social solidarity and a king would be unnecessary in such circumstances. The strength of the nation was proportional to the people's respect for the laws. Power was dispersed throughout the people rather than residing more visibly in an hierarchical arrangement culminating in a head of state. The legislature was ultimately a duty of the Levites. During the time of the Judges when as has been noted, the system seems to have worked as well as it ever did, the land rights of each family meant that power was essentially a local matter. The strength of the nation was aggregated from the power the local community derived from the landholding of all the local families. It was not so much the lack of central government that was important, rather that government was carried out by and through the individual citizen within their community. Each was to carry personal responsibility and to work along with others on community matters. To regard this absence of central government as 'anarchy' in a narrow pejorative sense does not

seem to fit the account. In the pre-monarchy days of ancient Israel the respect for the rights of all based on the ideal of *'love your neighbour as yourself'* kept the nation prospering, generally at peace and secure, and without central government. Recovery after periodic failures is witness to the robustness of the system.

A central authority can polarize dissension and threaten national unity, as was later to happen under the kings. For the young nation before the monarchy, power at the local level would usually present a strong deterrent to any hostile neighbouring countries. This would be in contrast to a situation with a centralized power structure which might be weak at the borders. Not that the nation prior to the monarchy was free from invasion. It is probable that the start of troubles with neighbouring nations, a regular feature of the time of the Judges, was triggered internally when the rich failed to fulfil the regulations and return land to the poor in the Jubilee year. Some people, threatened by oppression and maybe starvation since their land was not returned as was their right, went over to the alternative religio-economic systems of the neighbouring countries. In order to ensure survival and a good harvest these practiced child sacrifice to placate the fertility gods. The foreigners, seeing a disunited country, whose disaffected poor were becoming culturally dependent on them through religion, seized their chance and invaded. This gave rise to national action, and an Israelite military force gathered around a prominent leader who inspired the people to eject the invaders. But this leadership was only a temporary need and was non-sustaining, since the people disbanded afterwards, with the task done.

The rights within Moses' system were reinstated under the leader-judge as he or she headed the legislature and enforced the law. Peace reigned. In the story of Ruth, justice for Naomi and her family was dealt with locally by local people. Samuel although not a Levite by birth, went on a national circuit as a judge, going to the local need, which was easier than the people travelling to a central location. In contrast to Samuel's accessibility, judicial power became more concentrated after political power became centralized under the monarchy and ultimately focussed on one person when everyone travelled to King David for legal decisions. This concentration of power within a monarchy not only brought rougher justice because of the impossibility of one person being able to cope with the workload, but also made the usurpation of that power so much easier. Absalom his son, gained the support of the people by standing by the roadside in Jerusalem and belittling his father's decisions. With localized power guarded by the thousands of families all over the nation it was very difficult for the ambitious to grasp it for themselves, as was seen when Abimelech found that his self-imposed reign as king ended after three years, prior to the establishment of the period of the more lasting monarchy.

On legal issues that affected the whole nation the whole nation dealt with it, as seen in the case of the crime at Gibeah and the subsequent assembly at Mizpah. The handling of this case illustrates the dismay of the nation at some of their number opting out of the national decision making. Thus, whether in local or national matters of justice the people seemed to have had a real unity of purpose and an awareness of the responsibility that went with their family-held power.

Eventually however, the rise of corrupt judges and the hope that a king with an army might be a better solution to hostile neighbours than the ad hoc taking up of arms by all, brought a sea change in the national characteristics. The establishment of the monarchy was to lead to a loss of rights and responsibilities that the Mosaic checks and balances had established. Rights to slave and debt release, zero interest and rest years would eventually be forgotten. The enlightened principles that Moses had laid down and Joshua had followed, were increasingly ignored.

Everyday education - politics and economics
It was in the interest of each family to inform children of their heritage and educate them in the Mosaic paradigm, laws and regulations. The importance of their freedoms and rights, that is, the strong political element, figured strongly in the education of children at all times. As children enquired about the meaning of the laws the reply was to include the reminder about the powerlessness of their ancestors as slaves in Egypt. This was used as an object lesson in what might happen if they disregarded their amazing heritage, encapsulated in the laws. By contrasting the two situations and talking about the purpose of the laws, Moses instructed the people to make it clear that political freedom and the benefits flowing from it were dependent on obligations and duties. The laws were to be read out to all the people at the seven year breaks so that everyone, seven years old and upwards, would understand their heritage, rights and responsibilities.

*

E. UPDATE

Why are so many poor always with us?
Since its foundation 13 centuries after Moses, the Christian church, breaking out of the geographic confines of its Judaistic birthplace eventually became a major holder of wealth itself in most areas in which it became established. Its solution to poverty was largely through charitable hand-outs, even though this aspect of the Mosaic system was never intended to be more than an emergency measure. In England the long history of the enclosure of common land meant that many people could no longer subsist unsupported. The subsequent rise of poverty added to the need for more extensive organization for poor relief than the church could manage, and thus did governments become more involved in it. The church had lost sight of the principles of Moses whose teaching the early church father Ambrose had echoed in the 4th century. Ambrose said that the earth was to be a common benefit for all but that greed had made it the right of a few – the rich.

With the loss of such a radical viewpoint, at times the poor needed help to prevent starvation and the terms usually required work. But the measures had none of the far-sighted devices from Moses that would have re-established the poor. The Articles of Religion of the Church of England enacted in 1562 *(Book of Common Prayer)*, refer to the Law of Moses and in Article 7 specifically exclude any obligation to keep the civil precepts but do oblige people to keep 'moral commandments'. But, as noted, the individual 'civil precepts' of Moses' Law, such as those involving land ownership, were practical measures to enable people to treat each other according to the general 'moral commandments' as summarized by: *'love you neighbour as yourself'*. As the enclosure of the commons was well under way at this time and was depriving people of land which they had had time-honoured use of, this Article was a tacit acceptance of the enclosure movement despite the principles behind Moses' Law. However Article 28 does oblige everyone to be generous in giving charity to the poor. The failure to insist on a Mosaic solution concerning the land issue that could have resulted in new solutions for the dispossessed, meant that an increased number of poor had to be provided for by tithes, rents on church property and charitable donations. To turn society back to the enlightened principles behind Moses' Law from the usual Lottery Principle way of doing things, was clearly as difficult a task in Tudor politics as it might be today. The church was inextricably intertwined with the civil power, and being a major landowner itself was unable to address political issues from the Mosaic viewpoint of the individual in family groupings.

The foundational statements of The Articles combined with the financial status quo of massive landholdings has removed the influence of Mosaic thought on fundamental political matters in the English-speaking world ever since. The heavy burden of state welfare provision and private charity result from this. Despite a vibrant economy and a technologically successful society, the numbers of people on low, or no, income and needing help, still requires everyone else to contribute burdensome taxes to support them. Our palliative to the Lottery Principle is the *redistribution of income,* whilst Moses was more concerned with the *restoration of assets.* We deal with the symptoms of the economic failure of our sub-Mosaic system, rather than to re-establish the poor. We ignore the fundamental individual rights, economic mechanisms and awesome freedoms of Moses, which would eradicate a large amount of the poverty that so permanently endures. Individual compassion can achieve a little, but is inadequate to cope with extensive poverty. The need for a high level of welfare has to be managed by a powerful state and this confirms what Samuel said happens under the rule of a king 'you will become his slaves'. Slaves are usually given subsistence but they have limited rights and this describes life for many today. The surer way to relieve poverty long term, is to empower the suffering poor, by grafting into the economic system some basic economic rights for all.

Right and Left Politics

Many of the ideologies of our modern societies include some characteristics of the Mosaic paradigm, but deny others. Libertarians of the right might champion Moses' ideas of individual freedom as a foil against state power, and welcome the ad-hoc co-operation arising out of family and other groupings. But they might object to the regulations concerning regular and universally taken work breaks, because of the restriction of freedom to trade at all times (for example). But if freedom for the poor is not strictly safeguarded then the freedom achieved through wealth concentrates around those who have it.

On the other hand, the collectivists and socialist planner-controllers would welcome Moses' restoration of 'Free Lunches' to address poverty, but would vest ownership of that wealth in the state,

Jesus – rules and beyond rules

It had always been the hope under Moses that the Law would be 'written on minds and hearts' so that the regulations on economics and social issues would be observed and hopefully exceeded, in accordance with the spirit of Moses' phrase: *'love your neighbour as yourself'*. The biblical account tells how some, in their concern and commitment to others, did go further than the minimum demand of the law. Jesus, some 12 centuries after Moses, as a Jew and commentator on Moses, said he rejected nothing from this law and gave a new rendering of the Mosaic phrase with: *'do to others as you would have them do to you'*, known as the Golden Rule.

Indeed, the phrase most frequently quoted by Jesus and his followers from the writings of Moses and the Prophets was: *'love your neighbour as yourself'*. This emphasis underlines its importance to them as the normative statement of the Mosaic paradigm for society. It established that human relationships are still to be the foundation on which practical regulations and laws can be built. Jesus' emphasis of the importance of Moses' Law was that it would not disappear whilst human society existed. He foretold that the poor would always be with us, thus giving reason as to why the economic aspects of that Law would always be needed. But he broadened its traditional definitions of 'neighbour' to include all people, even enemies, as opposed to the old exclusiveness of race and nationality under Moses; and his attitude to retaliation as a means of justice was quite different.

As an indication of his acceptance of the Mosaic paradigm he used its financial language (debt forgiveness) to give insight to deeper truths about a more fundamental forgiveness. He used the phrase 'old treasure' to describe the Mosaic Law and said it was not to be neglected by his followers, who were to strive for co-operation and harmony. It remained as the indicator of minimum standards.

The new way for Jesus' followers in particular, was meant to lead to purer and greater self-sacrificial behaviour than the minimal standards of the Law. This new dynamic, reaches beyond the image of fair play in a game as per the old Law, to the kind of co-operation required in making music in an orchestra or band.

Purposes of rules

Jesus gave a practical illustration about looking for the purpose behind the old laws and rules. As he walked through someone's field and picked ears of ripe grain for the free meal that Moses had permitted travellers to take some 1300 years before, the purists criticised him for doing this on the Sabbath day. Picking grain was considered to be 'work', and they gave the Sabbath 'no work' rule precedence over the 'free food' rule.

Jesus retorted 'the Sabbath was made for man and not man for the Sabbath', the laws were intended to bring benefit, not burden. They were to bring freedom, choice and enjoyment to the society that used them. If someone had to go hungry in order to observe the Sabbath then the interpretation of the Sabbath rule was faulty.

controlled by an elite; both of which ideas are at variance with those of Moses. The paternalistic, controlling tendencies of the socialist mindset that tries to meet every individual need is ultimately impossible to work out, whilst encouraging dependency in those helped, and hindering creativity for those funding the help. It thwarts those who would like to help in more personal ways, by taking some of their wealth to fund the grandiose state plans.

Camel swallowing

Another telling observation from Jesus was about the tendency to partial 'do-goodery'. People thought that by observing certain rules rather carefully, they had achieved the full purpose behind the Law. The religious experts of the day had a highly sophisticated interpretation of the practice of tithing so that even garden herbs were carefully measured out and one tenth given to religious work.

Jesus responded to their failure to attend also to the big issues of the Mosaic law, such as justice and mercy, by saying that although they were adept at 'straining a gnat out of a drink' they were actually 'swallowing a camel'. Weightier issues were ignored in favour of the easy fix. (See Chapter 6 for examples of modern versions of 'camel swallowing').

Several issues are coming together today which could be addressed by the approach Moses took to fairness in society. It can be appreciated by people with or without religious belief. Despite our modern sophistication and technical advances, politically and economically, life is full of uncertainty for too many people. The way we run our society would never get anywhere near a court, pitch or board, if it was suggested it should be played as a game.

The suggestion is that principles derived from Mosaic teaching and law, could lead to the greatest game ever, with many more people than now joining in as fully participating players!

3

THE CITIZEN'S ROYALTY
(A modern antidote to the Lottery Principle)

The Alaskan Permanent Fund

EVERY ALASKAN CITIZEN is in receipt of regular Free Lunches, through the payment of an annual dividend from the Alaskan Permanent Fund (APF). The website of the Fund (See Appendix C) spells out the right that all Alaskan citizens of more than one year's residence share equally in the fund, whether child, adult, rich or poor, whether urban or rural dweller.

The spending functions of the Alaskan state are quite separate from the saving function of the APF, which invests mainly in equities and bonds. The Fund is ultimately in the control of all the people of Alaska. They voted it into being in 1976 and it is only they who can amend its constitution by vote. No executive, legislative or judicial action can change it or abolish it. A recent dividend was US$1964 per head (September 2000), with the total payment amounting to about £5500 for a family of four. There is no financial means test of any kind, citizenship is the only qualification.

The APF has grown since dividend payments to citizens started in 1982 at a real rate of return of 10% per annum. Some is retained to inflation-proof the fund, so that the purposes are fulfilled of providing income for the current generation whilst the oil lasts, and for future ones when it is depleted.

The wealth from an earlier oil bonanza in Alaska had gone solely into government coffers and when it was over people wondered what there was to show for it. Thus the APF was started with some of the proceeds from the new oil sales. Meanwhile, in the UK, the wealth from oil royalties from the huge UK oilfields continues to go the way they always have done: to the government, despite suggestions at the time for it to be diverted to citizens (Samuel Brittain 1995). The Alaskan scheme has been running for over twenty years and is very popular. It gives the 580,000 citizens the security that comes from the backing of the $25.7bn fund (unaudited value on 16 January 2002). The Alaskan people are positively engaged - even to the extent of special teaching aids so that children at every stage of their education can learn basic economic concepts in the context of the dividend that they all receive from the Permanent Fund every year. The Alaskans are clearly eager that the empowerment that the Fund brings to every citizen is not neglected through ignorance. The daily value of the APF and educational material is posted on the Internet. Having been placed within various stock, bond and property markets the value of the wealth fluctuates with those markets. Fund dividend payment amounts thus depend partly on the health of various national economies as well as on the current price of Alaskan oil.

The Alaskans are treating the natural resource of oil as Moses showed the people how to treat the natural resource of land – to be shared equally by all. Eventually the revenues will cease after the oil has been depleted, but the APF will hopefully continue paying out, because at least half the money is invested thus capturing value for future generations. Commercial firms, national or foreign, are not taking this part of the wealth, nor is it wasted on grandiose schemes by governments with more cash than they can handle. Individual citizens receive the money and choose how to handle it without conditions.

The Citizens Royalty (CR)

The example of Alaska is similar to the proposals of cash for citizens made by people like Thomas Paine, Henry George, C.H.Douglas, J.K.Galbraith, James Meade and others. This theme has been named variously: Citizen's Income, Basic Income, National Dividend and Universal Benefit. Milton and Rose Friedman named their rather different idea, Negative Income Tax. Citizen's Royalty is a new variation: '*Citizen*' tells clearly *who* the recipient is (rather than the other vaguer terms) and '*Royalty*' suggests a *right* due. The original idea of royalties and taxes paid to a sovereign, have long since been transferred to the state *on behalf of the people* and the Citizen's Royalty would bring some of this wealth back, *direct to the people*. '*Royalty*' also incorporates the idea of something that has at some stage been earned, whether through the ownership and exploitation of natural resources, personal skill or through work by preceding generations. The Citizen's Royalty would be a way that sophisticated post-industrial societies could incorporate fairer, citizen-centered, Mosaic principles. Clearly the idea of a Mosaic-type family plot of land for everyone is quite inappropriate for survival in our society and impossible to be administered fairly even if it was, but the CR, funded as described below, captures several important elements of the Mosaic idea. It would redress the natural tendency of an economy and society to work according to the Lottery Principle and would lift many people out of the poverty that ensues from its working. It is now being recognised by some that a basic income is the only way for a permanent improvement to be effected for the poor. It would encourage them into the productive economy, whilst at the same time resolving the problems of the increasingly complex benefit system in a simple and affordable way. In a similar manner to the Alaskan model, a fund for the management of CR payments could be established, named the Citizen's Royalty Fund (CRF), with the sources of income for this Fund as detailed below.

The payment of a standard CR amount, without means test, to every child and adult whatever their wealth status would benefit the poor proportionately more than the rich. In the UK we already have a Citizen's Income called Child Benefit (previously known as Family Allowance). It is a non-means tested payment benefiting the parents of every juvenile below 16 years old (and some below 19 years). Those on higher levels of income tax might initially be taxed on their Royalty. But as the Royalty grew in time it could replace tax allowances which could be phased out. Thus eventually no one would pay tax on it. A feature of the CR is that the disincentive for the unemployed to work, due to the loss of benefit pound for pound following any earnings, would be removed. The CR would be an irrevocable right to all whether working or unemployed, unlike benefit payments that can be effectively stopped through small earnings. Due to the demise of the 'job for life' there is an increasing need to aggregate income from several jobs, or sources, to build a living income, and the CR payment would help this. Existing benefit arrangements require ever more complex devices to counter their worst effects, one of which is to keep people in a non-working mode through the above disincentives. With a guaranteed small basic income there would open up choices for parents who currently need to farm out their children to child minders and go to work themselves. The current pressure from government to get everyone including parents of young children 'back to (employed) work' as soon as possible is contrary to one of the core values of the Mosaic family oriented paradigm. For many people the CR (or the CRs of several family members) might enable them to pay for someone in the family to care for an ageing relative rather than have to utilise expensive, non-family, commercial carers and be forced to fund this by having to take a job. The central advantage of the CR however is that choice is enhanced - it might pay for childcare, or be the means of making childcare unnecessary. The choice would be for the citizen to make.

The means testing of benefits encourages some to spend their income rather than to save to provide for later years. Those who are thrifty and self-reliant and accrue savings, exclude themselves from benefits on the account of their savings, whilst the spenders remain an expense of the state. The identical payment of the CR to all would give a small income to the spenders without punishing those who manage to save a little extra for a more comfortable retirement, since their savings would not be of any concern for the payment of the CR.

There would be a multiplicity of ways in which the Citizen's Royalty could be used apart from the family and caring orientated uses already mentioned. Whether: directly for living costs such as extra home heating or dining out; investing long term in a pension plan; running a car or van to find work or run a business; paying off debt; attending a college course; affording a holiday; having time to develop an artistic or musical skill or a craft; or funding charitable work - the possibilities are endless. Students for example, could find that their need to run up debt in order to study would be much reduced, or even eliminated especially if they saved some of their Royalty for a while before studying. But who needs help in deciding how to spend *their* money!

What amount would the Citizen's Royalty payment be?

The result of a political decision by government, depending on the available funding
(see the main text for suggestions)
In Alaska the dividend from oil royalties rose from
$386 per head in 1983 to $1963 in 2000

Apathy by voters about politics may stem from feelings of personal ineffectiveness about political matters and disillusionment with politicians. Resentment of, and frustration with, a system that encourages Chancellors of the Exchequer to devise more complex and stealthy ways to extract tax equivalent to around 40% of the national wealth, leads to greater polarisation, between politicians - *them* - and *us*. But the benefit of a CR would catch people's interest because it would give *us* (especially those of us with the greatest lack) a little more security and a little more choice than we had before. This should not be surprising to anyone who understands the power that comes with the Free Lunch principles of the Mosaic system.

The real power in that system was the people's power, as backed up by the law that gave individual and family rights. The CR could be the start of a similar idea in our own time. Opportunities are regularly being missed to bring power back to the people. What might turn the political apathy and frustration could be CR cheques dropping through every letterbox in the land.

What could I spend my Citizen's Royalty on?

It would be up to you to use your Royalty exactly how you wished. It would be available to spend, save or give away according to choice. It would be used like any other income: for ordinary daily expenses; for special expenses like a holiday; for savings; for a pension; for a hobby; for charity work, for education and training...the list would be endless because every one of us would choose differently.

The pity would be if Governments merely took the revenue-raising alternatives proposed below and used them just to bring in a bit more tax, without reducing or abolishing existing ones. There are choices as to what the taxation reform involved could achieve:
1. The replacement of revenue from other taxes
2. Extra government spending
3. Greater economic efficiency
4. Personal income through the Citizens Royalty.

The heart of our argument is that the empowerment of individuals (4) should be the priority accompanied by a promotion of improved economic functioning (1,3). Old and failing collectivist solutions (2) need to be replaced with new 'citizen based' solutions, such as the Citizen's Royalty to divide the Free Lunch benefits of nature, and of our society, more fairly between everyone through an actual regular 'Free Lunch' payment, to help encourage responsible citizenship.

The CR will not make anyone rich, it will not by itself provide a living income, but it will open up new possibilities for every citizen and especially for the poorest. Some of these differences will be purely material, but many people would find that their everyday lives are enriched in their relationships, and in other non-material ways, through this simple device. Introduced gradually and with care, to avoid inflation, it would replace some government spending. For a broad overview of the possibilities see *The New Economics of Sustainable Development* by James Robertson. (Appendix C).

The CR should not raise house prices if Land Value Tax (LVT, see page 40) was introduced at the same time or soon after. This should be taken into account by those who would introduce a citizen's income without LVT. The tendency for some of the new money from Citizen's Royalties to feed through into rising house prices would inhibit its purpose of benefiting the poor. Such a policy would act rather like the earlier tax relief on mortgage interest that added to house price inflation at booming times.

The Citizen's Royalty would not give the longer term additional benefit of land itself as an asset in our day on which to base a developing business or on which a dwelling could be built. But it would be similar in the Mosaic pastoral system to the value flowing from working the family land for survival purposes.

The Citizen's Royalty and less harmful taxation

The proposal is not only to use new sources of funding to pay for the Citizen's Royalty (see CRF Sources 1 to 7 in the main text), but also to reform taxation through reducing conventional taxes and eventually phasing some out altogether. Tax from the new sources encourages greater economic efficiency, when compared with income tax and VAT. This is an added benefit of reform quite apart from that of sharing nature's and society's wealth fairly via a Citizen's Royalty.

The new sources are generally *progressive* in that they are more affordable by those who have more wealth; and they do not burden the poor by charging tax on essential goods, which is a characteristic of *regressive* taxes. They do not, due to high levels of tax, harm the tax raising capacity of the tax source. However if any existing conventional taxes are still required, the Citizen's Royalty can be used as a means of ameliorating some of their *regressive* effects.

For example, if it is decided to continue the high taxation of motor fuels for ecological reasons so that the development of greener fuels is promoted, then some of the yield of the fuel tax could be added to everyone's Citizen's Royalty to compensate for the tax on a basic annual mileage. The green purpose of the high tax would be achieved, since heavy users of the fuel would be encouraged to change to cheaper, greener engines; but the poor would be protected against the *regressive* effects of the tax until such time as the cleaner fuels were more affordable to them.

Old mindset, New mindset

One of the difficulties in comparing the Mosaic model for the economy and for society, with our own, is the existence of the modern bureaucratic state and the affect it has on the lives and income of all citizens. It is so all-pervading that we tend to think that there can be no other way to run things; that we must accept as inevitable that millions will remain unemployed, many more will be in poverty and the state must look after them. But when looked at dispassionately, most people would surely agree that by any reasonable standard our socio-economic system has failed. We pay approximately 40% of the national product we create to the government and a large proportion of this is merely covering for the failure of the economy to enable many of us to survive on our own efforts. With this state of affairs seemingly so permanent it might appear bizarre to even consider the possibility of a Citizen's Royalty (CR) for every citizen. This shows how rooted we are in economic patterns and expectations which ignore such models as Moses' and the insights of the classical economists. We fail to take seriously campaigners like Henry George (see below), C.H.Douglas and more recently, James Meade, in advocating a National Dividend or Citizen's Income. These people and their enlightened ideas sometimes fail to get even a passing mention in textbooks on economics so lightly are their simple, yet radical, ideas regarded.

THE CITIZEN'S ROYALTY FUND (CRF)
Where would the money come from?

CRF income No. 1: Land Value Tax (LVT)
It was Henry George (1839-1897) the author of the best selling book on economics *Progress and Poverty (1879)*, who most clearly pointed out that every increase in prosperity leads to higher land prices which, through adding to housing costs, keeps the poor, poor. He wrote that 'This association of poverty with progress is the great enigma of our times'. We have over a century of evidence since his time to prove his point beyond any doubt. The lot of the poor, has improved in absolute terms, at the cost of a hugely bureaucratic and burdensome welfare state, but it does not lift their poverty relative to our prosperous society. George was a United States journalist, self-taught economist and politician, who, following on from the ideas of the French Physiocrats of the 18th century, the classical economists Adam Smith, David Ricardo, J.S.Mill and others, and from his own observations, proposed the introduction of a tax on land plot values. A tax on the value given to the land element of a site alone, after excluding all

value derived from any building or other improvements on it. Ideally the Land Tax was to be a Single Tax in place of all other taxes.

He showed that the value of land in any location is solely a result of the activity of everyone in the district, village, town, city or nation. The general prosperity that comes from *everyone's* combined efforts as a working community, feeds through into increased land values as people choose to put their increasing wealth into real property. But of course this *only* benefits those who actually own land, be they developers, pension funds, property firms or the ordinary freeholder of one house. The freeholder, whatever he or she may do to enhance their house *on the plot* adds nothing to the value of *the plot itself*, apart from their contribution as an individual to the general economic success of the surrounding community and nation. Thus are land values (as a component of house prices) a key indicator of the underlying success of a national economy. George proposed the imposition of Land Value Tax (LVT) or Site Value Tax, or Rating (SVT or SVR), to return some of this land value to the community, to pay for whatever services or facilities that the community needs, and also to fund a small citizen's income for all, which he called a National Dividend.

Mosaic parallels and contrasts
George's conclusions align well with the Mosaic principles. In Moses' system, as noted, a land sale price in any particular year was to be related solely, no more and no less, to the number of harvests remaining until Jubilee year. It would thus relate to the profit from the human work input on it and no extra value was to be demanded or paid. The increased value in land that we are so familiar with, within the 'soaring house prices', was banned. This meant, among other benefits, that spare wealth was not locked away in land values but directed to productive investment. What Moses banned, Henry George proposed to tax, so that the value of land should be released and provide for the common services and welfare for society. In Moses' simpler system these services were provided directly by each family for themselves and for others.

As this topic forms the subject of the chapters 4 & 5 an introduction only is needed here. Unlike oil revenues, land is a permanent resource for every country and land values will usually have a yield. Clearly land values do fall as well as rise, but prosperity continues beyond the occasional downward blip in economic growth and thus land always has value. There is not the need to conserve the value taken from land through LVT for the use of future generations, as is needful with oil in Alaska, since land does not get used up. It will always be there, essential and attracting wealth like a magnet, and as such always available to give up some of its value for LVT purposes, some of which could be immediately passed on to the Citizen's Royalty Fund and thence to the citizens via their regular CR payment.

The wealth within land has certain characteristics that are common to all the resources suggested for the funding of the CR. Firstly, the land resource occurs naturally but is in limited supply. Secondly it is essential to everyone for living, i.e. in high demand, and the limited supply means that high values are created. Thirdly, although everyone contributes to the successful society which automatically creates high land values, it is only some people who actually own this wealth. Many are left out, for example those who are renting a property to live in, rather than owning one. It is usual in free markets for prices to fall over time as goods gets cheaper due to competition between suppliers. Thus goods that were expensive luxuries when they are first on the market (like cars, refrigerators, televisions, etc.) become reasonably priced everyday essentials and the proportion of household spending on such items falls with time. But with housing costs (which represent for our purposes here, land costs) although spending per household might be easily affordable to new owners in economically quiet times it then rises again for later buyers, as economic growth feeds through into a land boom (the 'soaring house prices' of the headlines). This can be observed in the figures published concerning the percentage of an income spent on a mortgage, and the ratio of the average house price to the average income. Although certain areas do suffer long term economic decline and this takes land values down, most land values rise, are maintained, or rise again in time and again take an increasing proportion of household income. Such is a characteristic of prices in a monopoly situation. The poor, who can only rent, find that their rents follow land prices up so that the spending on housing of poor and richer alike rises together. With every upward swing of house prices new freeholders not only pay inflated prices for their own housing but, along with all taxpaying freeholders, pay for the housing welfare benefits of the poor too!

In Hong Kong where land values have been used to fund public services, those with average income or below, pay no income tax at all. The country has had a top ranking economy for many years, maybe this is due to money flowing into entrepreneurial activity rather than into land. What could LVT yield in the UK? Fred Harrison gives it as sufficient to cover all government expenditure (Appendix C. Harrison. 1998.). Clearly, if only a part of this was used and was added to other new sources of tax being discussed here, many of our existing taxes could be abolished.

Chapters 4 & 5 will deal in greater depth with land from other points of view. Having examined the modern equivalent of the Mosaic Free Lunch inherent in land values, the several extra sources of wealth that are available to contribute to the Citizen's Royalty (through modern civilisation), will now be investigated.

CRF income No. 2: Credit Reform (Seigniorage reform)

C.H.Douglas in the 1920s and '30s wrote concerning the difference between what he called real credit and financial credit (Mairet 1934). *Financial credit* is the one we are familiar with through the banking system. Its efficient operation depends on the ability of bankers to understand and service the *real credit* which exists only as a product of a successful society or community, as established over much time and maintained by the settled life of its citizens. The possibility of real credit, only arises through the productivity, skill and inventiveness of everyone who is, or who has been, part of the general success of that society up to that point. Real credit is an outcome of a stable society and is therefore truly the rightful wealth of all citizens, since they all make the society what it is. Moses banned interest charges on loans (no private profit was to be made for the *financial credit* given), thus keeping the society-generated Free Lunch (the real credit) available for all, at no charge. A modern equivalent of this is credit reform and joins Land Value Tax as a similar device achieving similar ends. Land values and real credit both arise from the same stable societies; they flourish where people create a community or society or nation; they may not exist at all in war zones where the fabric of society is breaking down. They are the products of the peaceful and creative efforts of every citizen, rich or poor alike. Everyone is rewarded appropriately for their own work and business acumen through wages and profit, but the Free Lunch benefit of credit creation taken by some represents an unfair appropriation of the common wealth. In *Creating New Money* (Appendix C. Huber and Robertson. 2000), the authors explain how money is created in our society. What Huber and Robertson propose is seigniorage reform. Historically it was the right of governments to issue coins and notes for currency purposes. Today very little of the money in circulation is in this traditional form; most money only appears as numbers in accounts, on screen, or at times on paper, and most of it is created by banks. Through the device called 'fractional reserve banking' banks can create money 'out of nothing'. If they have a customer who wants a loan of £1000 they do not need to find another customer who will make a deposit of £1000 to balance the new loan. Providing their reserves are at a certain minimum fraction of their total lending as set by the banking authorities, which could be less than 5%, and their customer satisfies their loan criteria, they just make the credit available and start charging interest. Banking rules to limit the completely free creation of unlimited amounts of money are complex, but the authors say that the banking system as a whole is able to match both sides of its business quite readily.

Bank customers receive a yield on their interest-bearing deposits of say 4%, but any money the bank lends out will yield the bank, say at least 9%. Some loans *are* matched by the interest bearing deposits, but not all of them by any means, and in their absence the newly created money makes a profit from the entire 9% or more.

What the banks are doing is making use of the supply of Douglas's 'reserve of energy' or 'dynamic capacity', or *real credit* in society, and capturing the advantage for themselves by charging interest. In terms of Mosaic Law, as noted, this was illegal because it denied people something that was to be available at no charge for those who needed it. Otherwise it would have added to the wealth of those who had it at the expense of those who were poor. The reform proposed by Huber and Robertson is that the central bank should be given some degree of independence from government and make the money that government and society needs. The government would be given what it needed for public spending, free of interest charges. The commercial banks would be charged at wholesale rates for the money they needed for their customers. By giving control and responsibility to the central bank over the supply of money it would also curtail the temptation of some governments to unwise spending.

As no interest would be charged by the central bank to the government, there would be drop in the funding of government through this saving of interest currently charged by the banks. U.S. presidents Thomas Jefferson and Abraham Lincoln advocated that the power to issue money should be taken from the banks and restored to the people. Huber and Robertson do not envisage that central banks will be able to create all the money governments need, due to the dangers of inflation, so it will not eliminate entirely all government borrowing from banks at interest.

When dealing with retail customers the banks would borrow from

Bakers and Bankers

These both supply things that are essential to life as we know it.
Bread the staple of physical life, and credit the staple of commercial life.

Just as everyone must pay for the bread they buy,
so everyone who borrows money must pay interest on it.
Whether they are an individual with a mortgage, a business investing in a factory,
or a government building a hospital, either directly or by the Private Finance Initiative.

From a pound of flour a baker will make one loaf.
But if you have £1000 in your bank account
a banker is permitted to lend £20,000 to other people
on the strength of your deposited money

The baker's profits is related to the volume of bread sold.
Every extra loaf sold brings the baker more profit,
after he has paid for the extra flour needed

The banker's profit is related to the volume of money lent at interest.
But having paid interest on your £1000 deposit
he charges interest on the newly created £19,000 at no cost.

Such a banking system is only possible in peaceful and law-abiding societies.
In troubled societies and in uncertain times too many people would want their
deposits back at one time to enable the system to work so easily.

So bankers can only create multiple loans out of tiny deposits because
of the successful society we all manage to create.

It is natural justice that people be rewarded for the work they do.
Such as bakers for breadmaking, lawyers for advising and artists for pictures.

Since then, it is all of us together, and not bankers, who create the essential conditions
needed for such an ingenious credit system to flourish,
should it not be us, collectively, who receive the reward?

Whilst we all need to pay interest on money we borrow personally,
why should our government pay interest on the money it needs,
as it provides the things we democratically decide we need?

The main text explains how governments, rather than bankers,
could create money free of interest, thus reducing costs of government,
lowering taxes, and even providing a regular Citizen's Royalty for all.

the central bank, pay interest on this money and then lend it on as usual. We would still make the same payments for our mortgages. But the profit from credit creation will have been diverted from the private enrichment of a few, back to everyone in society, who merely by being part of that successful society made that particular wealth possible. Since credit is essential for our economic system the savings could represent a substantial part of the funding of government spending or contribute to a Citizen's Royalty. The authors estimate that the money system reform measures that they propose, would yield enough to cut 12 pence in the pound off income tax; or fund 15% of the current national tax bill (Huber & Robertson. 2000). Alternatively, using their figures, an annual Royalty payment of up to £800 could be made to all 60m UK citizens.

The three characteristics concerning wealth from credit creation are very similar to that from land. Firstly, credit is a product which arises out of a stable human society (rather than, in the case of land, occurring naturally), but it is limited in supply for reasons of sound monetary management. Secondly, credit is essential to everyone and the demand brings certain and steady profits to those who can supply it. Thirdly, although everyone contributes their part in making the prerequisite for credit creation, the settled society, it is only the banks which take the profits from this communal success.

CRF income No.3: New technology – radio spectrum
The sale of the new 'third generation (3G)' mobile phone licences in 2000 raised £22.5bn, which immediately disappeared into the government pot. This could have been a one-off payment of a Citizen's Royalty to 60 million citizens at £375 per head, i.e. £1500 for a family of four. These are natural resources, newly available, and the proposal involves no debate about the redistribution of wealth (as would be the case with LVT or credit reform). The device simply raised new money from capitalists who were willing to part with it as they proceed to make a profit.

Yet the government unimaginatively adjusted a few figures on the national balance sheet, and carried on as though nothing could have been any different. The impression is given that this is the only way to manage things. 'Government knows best how to spend the nation's (your and my) resources', seems to be the unquestioned dictum. No wonder people are apathetic about politics when politicians can miss such amazing chances of empowering them.

Yet again, the three characteristics of the wealth available through these new resources are as before: firstly, the resource is naturally occurring but limited, as only one supplier can use one waveband at a time to achieve orderly broadcasting. Secondly the resource is in great demand in modern society, and this creates value for those who are granted the licence who then can satisfy the demand from the public. Thirdly, and in this case as an improvement on the way we treat land and credit wealth, the Free Lunch wealth has actually been captured for the public good and is directed to the public purse. The auction successfully extracted high value from the suppliers who were very willing to pay high prices because they expected that high profits would flow over the licence period.

CRF income No.4: Mineral royalties
As has been mentioned, Samuel Brittan with Barry Riley in 1978 suggested that the state's oil revenues under the North Sea be handed directly to citizens, as per the Alaskan example, (Brittan. 1995). Now over twenty years later, still no such thing has happened, no Citizen's Royalty Fund or anything like it has been created to channel this wealth from new leases that arise or old ones that are renewed. The decades pass and the chance of building up the income of families and individuals from this source disappears as steadily as the oil is depleted.

The oil or other mineral wealth occurs naturally. These are commodities in high demand for modern life and this creates the high value. But in these cases the government is actually capturing some of the wealth for the benefit of society through the state machine, even though not individually and directly for citizens.

CRF income No.5: Privatisations
Samuel Brittan also suggested handing out the UK privatisation shares free to citizens (Brittan. 1995). South Africa at the time of writing plans to allow every citizen to buy a small number of shares in the state owned telecoms company at a price which reflects only the administration cost of that part of the privatisation exercise. Institutional and other investors will pay the full market price. A Citizen's Royalty Fund is another way of handling such a distribution, so that the proceeds provide an Alaskan-style share and bond portfolio, only retaining sufficient of the original companies for a balanced portfolio. Someone said that the privatisation procedure was like 'selling the family silver', but to set up a CRF would have been to pass the sale proceeds back directly *to everyone in the family* via the

CR payments. The privatisation exercise usually extends disparities of wealth, as only those able to buy the shares gain an asset and income. This is not to criticise the idea as such, only that the publicly created assets were sold off cheap to a selection of citizens. Another opportunity to bring Free Lunches to all was missed. The Lottery Principle held sway yet again, with the rich moving ahead, their new wealth based on the past efforts of everyone, with the poor left standing or, relatively speaking, slipping back.

CRF income No.6: Conventional sources, Intestacy proceeds

Conventional taxes, if they continued as part of state fund raising, could contribute to the CRF, after meeting other needs. The proceeds of intestacy, although small, could with justification be placed in a CRF, rather than be 'lost' in general government spending.

CRF income No. 7: Green Taxes (Ecotaxes)

The pressure to conserve natural resources brings calls for taxes on energy use in order to force people to economize. But these taxes have an unfortunate effect on the poorest since they cannot do without a certain minimum amount of petrol, heating oil, gas, electricity, etc. Economies may be impractical for them and they will be impoverished by such environmentally well-meaning measures. This regressive taxation, can be countered if a CR system is in operation, by adding part of the Ecotax yield to the CR payment to cover a basic minimum usage of the resource, thus cancelling out the negative effect tax for everyone's essential use. This would work for minimum essential motoring use, heating use and so on. Thus would the plight of the poorest be addressed without the cumbersome means tested benefits of current welfare. At the same time pressure would be on all to reduce energy use.

A similar tax, a daily charge for bringing vehicles into congested city areas, when set merely as a tax, favours the rich to whom the charges are of little consequence. The less wealthy who need to come into town just as much suffer relatively more and may not be able to pass the charge on to others. If some of the yield of such charges were recycled as a local element within CR payments, perhaps such town traffic pricing schemes would become more widespread to the benefit of the people in and around towns. The charging for road use cuts against the element of the Free Lunch associated with public rights of way. Free passage over roads has been taken for centuries as a basic right of every citizen. As such it has been a Free Lunch with intrinsic value only, being given no monetary value until congestion charges are made. To embark on these schemes without introducing some means of recompensing those who have to enter such streets as part of their daily life, is to push the poorest further into their poverty. The use of a Citizen's Royalty in this connection is an ideal way to safeguard the poor.

Another ecotax that could contribute to the CRF, is that of charges for aircraft landing slots, these are similar to entry charges for congested towns. Certain times of day, and different seasons and airports would fetch different prices and auctions could be the way to capture the value of this society-inspired wealth for the Fund. It might also help to promote the more efficient use of existing airports and thus possibly delay the building of new runways at certain airports whilst others are underused.

Free Lunch Wealth
How it happens and who gets it

- It arises from resources that are either naturally occurring (like land, minerals, radio waves), or that a successful society generates (like credit and money creation, or rights of way). These resources are usually limited in supply

- They are vital to modern living, and being in high demand are valuable.

- The resulting wealth from those given a monetary value, is usually held unevenly across society and many people are left out. This is despite the fact that the high values arise through *everyone's* combined success in creating the society that needs the resources.

*

It is basic justice, therefore, to use this wealth, through taxing it,
to provide for the services and facilities that society needs
and to provide a Citizen's Royalty for every citizen.

What's in the national piggy bank? How the Fund would work.
The website for the Alaskan Permanent Fund (see Appendix C) is a superb model for its transparency and comprehensiveness. The ability of governments to control what they want the general public to see and what they want to hide, is not possible with the Alaska Fund since the APF is quite independent of government. A Citizen's Royalty Fund with actual value like the Alaskan Fund would bring Governments and political parties under pressure to maximise the CR

payments. Voters would find that they have a new influence on policymakers. Many budget issues would become so much clearer than they can be now, when stealth taxes are slipped in and the government spending machine swallows them up quite invisibly to the ordinary voter and, almost certainly, very wastefully.

There is great pressure for the government to improve public services. The 'solution', so often is to spend more money. Politicians with huge sums of money, managing gargantuan organizations, cannot handle resources in the same careful way that most households or individuals can handle them. If every citizen received a Citizen's Royalty, the money would be spent on whatever *they* chose, rather than as now by government decision; and it would, among other things, bring market sensitivity into some services that are currently subject to bureaucratic planning.

4

LAND AS A WEALTH MAGNET
(How the Lottery Principle works with land)

Wealth magnets

Natural resources such as land, oil, gas and radio waves can be likened to magnets that attract the wealth of a society in the way a natural magnet attracts iron filings. Land in particular is such a device and is almost without challenge in the medium and long term for its low risk and virtual certainty of increase in value.

The more successful the community, the more desirable the surroundings, the more settled the times and the more law abiding the citizens, the greater the value of land wealth, whether on the local or national level. The value of all the land of a nation is a good indicator of the success of all its citizens in creating a thriving society. Whilst for many this land wealth is locked away and lying idle, increasingly people who are sitting on good gains remortgage the property and spend some of the gain. But renters have no such private store of wealth to tap into.

For us in a post-industrial society, land is just as personally essential to everyone for accommodation, even if it is not so now for food as it was in a pastoral society. Property is usually in steady demand and this is proved by the climb in property prices, which reflect the underlying rising land values. We can never return to a simple pastoral society, but we need to recover the principle that everyone should have a right to the wealth that is represented in the land values. This is simply because everyone makes their own contribution to the thriving society that gives rise to the increasing values.

Adam Smith, the founding father of modern economics (1723-1790) advocated the levying of a tax on land values to raise funds for public expenditure. He wrote that the high value associated with building land was particularly appropriate for such taxation since its values were derived from, in his terms: the 'good government of the state', or in our terms: the part that everyone plays in making a prosperous society. He recommended that the land on which a building was placed should be taxed separately to the building itself, and noted that it should not be difficult to distinguish the two. Before proceeding further we need to note a particular aspect of his writings.

He stated that the land of uninhabited houses should not be taxed, on the grounds of hardship to the owner. Since this concession would have had the effect of protecting the owner of the land from the market pressures that others were under, he is seen here as protecting certain monopolists, which he readily acknowledged all owners of land to be. This is at variance with the anti-monopolist principles that he championed in other markets, wherein the benefits of lower prices and improved services and goods might come to all, through competition. After all why should the owner of an empty house be protected whilst waiting for a higher rent or sale price in rising markets? Whatever the reason for the vacancy, in not being required to pay tax on the land the owner would be a protected monopolist at a time when other owners were forced to pay. Such a concession would be unjust, open to abuse, reduce the benefits of market conditions and would probably render a land tax impractical.

If an entrepreneur decides to market a desirable new product, good profits will flow since the product will command a high price due to the temporary monopoly enjoyed. This is what happens in such crazes as the plastic Hula-Hoop or the Rubic Cube. But a free market ensues (allowing for the short term protection afforded by patents), as others start to produce similar products, and the extra supply causes prices to drop whilst increasing consumer choice. The original entrepreneur receives good rewards through being first in the market, but gradually these reduce through competition which breaks the monopoly. The long-term history of prices of manufactured goods clearly indicates that where we enjoy free markets, competition brings reductions in prices, and an increase in variety and choice.

This is not so with land. In the land market there is no natural mechanism which is equivalent to free market competition for goods and services, which would, by encouraging extra supply, moderate land values, and make land more affordable over time. Because the supply of land where people can live is limited and because new houses cannot be built fast to respond to demand, land prices react with high volatility, with swings up, and more briefly, down, and are very different to figures for general inflation. There is very little of the flexibility that is natural to other freer markets, where prices and supply tend towards an equilibrium as demand is satisfied. Whereas a vital key to a manufacturer's success is *action*, a land or property owner often gains through *inaction*, keeping property off the market awaiting a higher price. A house or office building can be boarded-up for years and gain much value - quite the reverse of the manufacturer who needs to rush goods to market before others flood in and force the prices down. In the 1960's a new office building called Centre Point in London's Oxford Street remained empty for years whilst there was a pressing housing shortage. The owners enjoyed the Free Lunch through the increasing value of their land, and the shortage of housing was not relieved as it might have been by conversion from office use. The introduction of Land Value Tax would concentrate the minds of those who hold such accommodation off the market and would bring much empty space into use. Without the tax, whether we are freeholders or renters, we are all paying more than we need for the privilege whilst some owners keep buildings empty and land undeveloped, whilst values soar.

The failure of the planning system to moderate the wealth magnet effect of the land and housing market and the consequent effects on prices and affordability is the subject of the next chapter.

The hidden cost. No choice but to pay.

Whether you live in a sumptuous mansion, an ordinary family house or a tower block, one thing that you cannot avoid is the effect on your finances of the value of the land on which your dwelling sits.

Land costs take a substantial part of your household budget. Did you know that they are the first part of the cost you have to bear? They come before the bricks and mortar of the house itself; before the food, water, clothing, heating and lighting you need; and well before such things as the TV, telephone and other aspects of modern life. Not that the cost of land is ever shown as a separate item on your household bills, rent demands or building society mortgage statements. It is hidden from you within these other charges, but its effect is substantial for every single household and business, whether you are renting or buying a property. Land costs are also a factor in high taxes, as the cost of poverty relief is inextricably linked to high land values, as we shall see later.

Land costs are a huge factor in our modern economy whose importance is rarely acknowledged. The homeowner can get an idea of the value of their land by deducting the insured value of the building shown on their insurance policy from the price that similar houses are now selling for in the neighbourhood (Appendix A).

The land and the house

'House' prices always seem to be high, and are usually going higher. First-time purchasers struggle to get funds together for a deposit and then have to commit a substantial part of their income to pay off a mortgage, for over 25 years or more. But the asset they are pouring their effort and money into, brings no income in the manner of many investments such as a deposit account, shares or bonds. The value of the *building* is a product of such things as current wage and material costs, the expense of connecting up to gas, electricity and water supplies, and fees to the local authority and to architects. As a capital asset it will need constant maintenance and periodic refurbishment. Thus as soon as it is built its value gradually starts falling through deterioration and in the longer term through its lack of the most modern facilities. However the price of homes will usually show a substantial gain in value over time (as a look in an estate agent's window or the newspaper property pages proves), simply because the land on which the building sits is gaining in value. So the stories of soaring house prices are in reality not that at all, they are soaring land prices. Building land is a commodity relatively fixed in supply and when subject to sudden changes in demand experiences periodic climbs and crashes in price levels.

Details of the various costs involved in buying a home can be seen in Appendix A, but the following is a brief summary. Suppose someone buys an average property for £90,000 and they take out a 100% mortgage for 25 years. Over that period they will pay about £158,000, assuming an average real interest rate over the period of 5%, and will fully own the place at the end. This total sum works out at about 8 years of gross income for an average earner on £20,000p.a. The cost of the 'bricks and mortar', amounts to 3 years of income, and the interest and land costs, to 5 years of income. The value of a plot of land big enough for house and garden but *without* planning permission to build (valued for agricultural use), will be about £200. The value *with* permission for a house, will be about £30,000. This leap in value from £200, a 15000% (x150) increase shows the huge profit available to the original developer on the grant of planning permission. The monetary gain of £29,800 shows the extraordinary Free Lunch potential of land. This value is referred to technically as 'economic rent', or 'surplus value', and its high figure demonstrates the demand for building land. Its size is affected by the desire people have to live in convenient and desirable locations. The cost of the land with interest amounts to over £2000 each year, or about £176 monthly over the whole 25 year period.

For comparison with that other property related cost of Council Tax, the tax on an average house (a 'Band D' property) might be about £900 p.a. It helps to pay for services such as the police, waste collection, fire fighting, recreation and so on, and at £67 monthly it is about one third of what the land is costing.

The housing cost commitment of some first-time buyers at the 1990 peak for property prices reached 71% of take home pay. These people saw that property prices were running away from their ability to afford them and made a huge financial commitment to jump on the bandwagon. But a rapid drop in the number of new buyers caused property prices to slip and then to crash as the bubble burst. Prices took six or seven years to recover even the money values of the peak, and even a decade later, because of general inflation, in some areas, values were still below the peak in real terms, so the 'investment' has been poor for those who bought at the top.

Land & House

It is very obvious what we are buying in terms of bricks, mortar, kitchens and bathrooms when we purchase a home. The cost of building a house varies across the country, with London building prices possibly 20% higher than remoter areas.

The difference in land values due to different locations can be observed by comparing the asking price of a particular house and garden in London, with a similar sized one in an area 200 miles away. Even allowing for the slightly higher building costs associated with the London area, the difference in value shows how London land values can be a multiple of the land value of the distant ones. This illustrates that land in London and the South East of England has a more powerful 'wealth magnet' effect than land elsewhere.

Timing can be quite crucial. If you buy at a peak, then you may be caught for years with less value than you are paying for. Delay at the 'wrong' time and you may be priced out of the market altogether as it keeps zooming up beyond your reach. Delay at the 'right' time and you may be able to afford a bigger property in a year or two. This shows the nature of the housing market to be speculative and it is a wise precaution in any speculative market not to use money that you need to live on, as there are too many uncertainties. The early 1990's became a desperate time for nearly a million people who lost their homes and gathered heavy debt through the failed speculation that they seemed to have little choice but to make.

The everyday activity of buying a house locks income away very inaccessibly and this stored wealth is heavily represented by the land value. Those who trade in 'property' as a business, stand to make enormous profits if they get their timing right, selling near the top and buying again after the collapse. Whilst the cycle is climbing, many people find that they are living on land which is gaining more each month than the amount of their pay cheque.

But eventually the economy falters and the supply of people who have been putting their rising income into better homes slows up. Many people start to feel the pinch as their jobs become less secure. They become more and more financially stretched. The housing market starts to stick despite the efforts of developers to extend the choice by building smaller and smaller homes to make them affordable to the least prosperous buyers. The market grinds to a halt, prices reverse and the pyramid collapses. Those householders who bought just when prices were at a peak, find that the amount they have borrowed is now bigger than the sliding value of their property - the dreaded 'negative equity'. The cost of higher interest rates can compound the difficulties and some will have their homes repossessed by the lender because their income will not stretch enough; or they become jobless in the growing recession that is so strongly linked to the crash of the housing market. They will be left with no home of their own and, or, a large debt. What could have been a monetary Free Lunch asset has become a debt and what should have given satisfaction though the intrinsic Free Lunch value of home ownership has turned into a nightmare. These are the diners in the Free Lunch Restaurant of Chapter 1 whose meal makes them sick.

For those others who manage to cling on, the recession eventually turns into boom again, incomes climb and the loss may be eliminated. Financial uncertainty for people buying on mortgage can be a feature of home ownership especially in the early years. The housing market is notorious for its swings, which defy prediction. Besides most homebuyers usually need to start or change house ownership due to their personal circumstances without regard to the state of the market.

Who gets a Free Lunch?
With such rises in value many people may appear to be getting a Free Lunch. However whilst the intrinsic benefit of having your own home is its own reward, the financial Free Lunch is locked away in the land the house occupies. There are refinancing possibilities available to release cash, but for most, until this value is released on sale it is only a potential Free Lunch. A move into a smaller house, or into a cheaper area can release money for an income-producing investment. But many people would prefer not to have to move merely for this reason. For personal, family and work reasons there are great benefits from the network of relationships and local knowledge that have been built

up over years of settled life in one locality. On retirement it may be more possible to release equity from the asset by trading down in house size; but to *have* to move far away at a time in life when the need for increased personal support starts to grow, can be disruptive. State welfare is becoming ever more narrowly targeted and the benefits of well established, personal, local links and relationships will be increasingly invaluable in these circumstances.

There is another problem with the notion of trading down to provide income, and that is that this option offers less scope to those with houses at average value and below. The Free Lunch is effectively locked up in the high land value of their home for their whole lifetime even after they have finished paying their mortgage. There would be little spare equity left after downsizing, after the expenses of selling, buying and moving. For them the Free Lunch is there (the land wealth), but it is like a course of a meal in a restaurant brought in on a trolley, but merely to be looked at, and not consumed. The average monthly land cost of £176, as in the example (Appendix A) might just as well have been buried in a hole in the back garden for all the financial Free Lunches it is going to bring in. These might be the Free Lunch Restaurant diners who find that their Free Lunch has cost them dearly. Whilst the owner's children may benefit through an inheritance, those unable to trade down, whilst they do enjoy the pleasure of their own property, in financial terms are little different from the renters who gain no Free Lunches of any sort.

What is clear is that the Free Lunch of land wealth, which was in a pastoral society was the bedrock for survival and for wealth development for everyone, is, in our society, disproportionately available for those wealthier than the average. The property pyramid *inevitably* transfers wealth to the richer. If property generally rises 10% in a year the £90,000 property will rise £9,000 in value and the £500,000 one will rise £50,000. Thus is the value of the potential Free Lunch far greater for the wealthier than for the poorer. The many different participants in the property market are locked together; they are dependent on each other, but those who own higher value properties gain a lot, whilst many others gain very little that is financially useful. The poorer are enriching the wealthier, by being in the same property pyramid, and first time buyers contribute the most effort for the greatest risks - yet another demonstration of how the Lottery Principle works.

As the theme develops ways will be suggested by which the Free Lunch in land might be transformed into accessible wealth for all

The house-buyer's pyramid scheme

The housing market can be seen as bearing similarity to pyramid schemes that collect joining fees but sell no products. Some of these are illegal and can bring large fines or even imprisonment for those who set out to con the public. They work as long as newcomers keep arriving with new money which gets recycled up the pyramid to the benefit of those on board already.

No one has to join such a money game: they are for the gullible and the desperate. But with housing we have no choice. People cannot wait, they have to live somewhere – now; and so they join the 'house-buyers pyramid scheme' always hoping that the boom will carry on long enough for them to make good gains in value before the market grinds to a halt and prices fall back.

A feature of the soaring housing market in the new millennium was the rise in 'buy-to-let' deals being done, helped by low interest rates and the poor record of the stock market. People who already had a house, perhaps with high equity itself, entered the market again for renting out. The rents (assuming continuous occupancy) should cover the mortgage payments and maintenance, but the big carrot is the likely future rise in value of the underlying property.

Many of the houses in question are of the size and type normally sought by first time buyers. This buy-to-let activity helps to price such people out of the market.

Alan Greenspan on housing equity release

Those who own their own homes and have seen a rise in value can very simply re-mortgage and release some of the equity gain to spend on what they want. Alan Greenspan, Chairman of the Federal Reserve (the central banking system of the United States), said in London in September 2002 that such activity was important to the buoyancy of the economy of the time.

However, such choice is only available to those who are homeowners. Without the backing of the property asset, renters will have difficulty borrowing at all, and if they do it will be at least double the interest rate the mortgager has to bear. Also, their loan will need to be repaid much sooner. Renters not only do not have the pleasure of owning their own home but have no such nest egg 'on tap' to top up their spending.

A reform to use Land Value Tax to fund a Citizen's Royalty would distribute the property gains fairly and evenly. It would operate as a housing equity release scheme for every citizen. Just as renters no less than owners contribute to the gains because they are part of the economic success that generates house price gains, so they should share the rewards.

rather than locked away for most. What is preferable? Wealth *possibly* accessible in about thirty years after a lifetime of costly mortgage payments, or *usable* wealth now with reduced housing costs?

Council House sales and the need for subsidised housing

Since 1979 1.4 million council houses have been sold to tenants at discounts proportional to the length of their tenancy up to that point. Here is a feature that aligns well with Mosaic principles of Chapter 2 since it gives assets to those who generally have few assets. Yet all taxpayers have supported the housing subsidy of council-financed homes, but only some of the tenants have benefited, although the beneficiaries have, in this case, been targeted with some social justification. The benefit of the switch from public to private ownership is a gain to society in that it encourages people to make their own choices and to become responsible for more of their own affairs. The large discounts given to some purchasers should have protected them from negative equity through any downswing of the property cycle soon after their purchase. The negative effect of these sales is that a large amount of subsidised housing has been removed from the use of the poorest. To counter this, most new housing schemes of any size now require the developer to include a certain number of 'affordable homes' as a condition of planning consent. Builders and developers are thus compelled to carry out public policy on an ad hoc basis, site by site, through pressure from the local authority. Such schemes show that free market principles alone can never bring simple and fair solutions for housing. A better answer must be found which reduces the need for 25% of all housing to be subsidised at all (see Chapter 4).

The 'double-whammy' for renters

Those who rent property have no financial interest in land and do not benefit from any aspect of its rise in value. They are additionally hit by the need to continue paying rent for the whole of their lifetime, which inevitably rises along with the background rise in freehold prices. A house-buying neighbour's mortgage will end after 25 years or so, which will reduce their regular expenses at a time when they might have a reduced income, having retired; but the renter has no such help. Those in subsidised rented accommodation are likely to be on low earnings and unlikely to have saved to provide extra pension, so the chance of producing income to match the increased cashflow of the freehold neighbour when their mortgage payments cease, is unlikely. The Free Lunch from land values is never for those who rent housing, only for owner-occupiers and landlords.

Why does the Free Lunch from land value arise?

The practice of clearing people off common land by enclosing it for more profitable farming is an interesting pre-industrial development which illustrates our theme. What the common land provided up to then, was its ability to give many families the status of semi-independent smallholders, a distant throwback to the time of the Mosaic Free Lunch for all. But enclosure transferred the Free Lunch benefits inherent with working the common land from widespread shared use into fewer hands, and often with little or no compensation for the lost benefit. Gradually the need for agricultural workers declined due to more efficient methods, but labour demand associated with the new industries rose, thus there was a need for urban housing land. The price of the land for such housing would rise either to the most that a factory owner could afford to provide tied housing, or what workers could afford to rent or to buy for themselves. As time passed industries changed, and the siting of the new industries close to a workforce needing income was convenient, even if the geographical imperatives of power supplies or communications routes of the earliest factories receded. Thus was the land value of the housing maintained through a continuity of employment.

Who doesn't get the Free Lunch from land values?

According to Land Registry figures the price of an average London house in March 2000, was £163,300, having risen from £132,600 a year earlier - up 23%. London was enjoying prosperity with the result that some of those with increased income bought better houses. This is inevitable and automatic: house prices rise as the economy grows and the wealth gap between rich and poor increases because house prices rise faster than the incomes of the poor.

But as was asked in Chapter 1 who makes London successful? It is not only the heads of successful firms and the city wheeler-dealers, it is also the street cleaners, bus drivers, the police, waiters, teachers, nurses...everyone who works and lives there. London would not function if they were not there! Where would house values be then? But whilst all contribute to the long-term well-being of the metropolis, some will have been priced out of the housing market by the rise.

Let us assume that the financial wizards who earned good salaries and bonuses probably live in sought-after areas and in above average sized houses. Detached homes showed a 66% rise in value. The average flat rose from £117,000 to £166,300 and so new teachers, for example, earning around £22,000 p.a. could not have bought one even at the beginning of these rises. These figures show that the Free Lunch in land values is likely to be captured by those who have wealth already.

These who do not own their own home, but who need to be in London, where the jobs are, have no such Free Lunch 'scheme'. As mentioned before, the teachers who are building the future of the children of those people who are gaining an increasing Free Lunch from the rising value of their desirable homes, are unable to buy the smallest property for themselves. The same goes for nurses, the police, street cleaners, and the millions who makes London what it is. Their earnings do not rise fast enough to keep pace with the rising property prices, but their contribution to the prosperity is as essential as anyone else's. Their relative poverty *increases* with every upward move of the housing market and adds to the pressure for high wage claims as the firefighter's dispute of 2002/03 showed.

The government has a housing subsidy scheme for certain of these groups. This creates a new kind of elitism where only certain people are designated as 'key workers'. Besides, do nurses or teachers, really want to be housed together in an 'elitist ghetto' of tied houses, as some such schemes can create?

The interest rate roller-coaster
What makes house-buying in the UK especially uncertain is the way that most housing finance, which is a long term commitment, is linked to short term interest rates. These fluctuate rapidly and bring a chaotic, uncertain factor into what should be a relatively trouble-free and low risk transaction. People need to borrow to their income limit to have any chance of home purchase, and can get caught by an increase in interest rates. Rate guarantees only protect buyers for limited periods and these are at the expense of those not so guaranteed. If interest rates fall they can add to the speed of house price rises as people find they can afford to bid property higher. Thus lower interest rates do not help to make houses more affordable for long. Prices still run away.

Anti-social behaviour?
In the area of industrial relations, some trade union activity such as striking might be deemed to be anti-social behaviour, as employees disrupt production or essential services as they use *inactivity* in the

labour market in pursuit of their cause. *Inactivity* also benefits land and property traders as they pursue profits; but no social stigma attaches to this, which maintains the land market's endemic volatility and results in the high proportions of income being locked away in land value for every home purchaser and renter. No one would expect landowners and freeholders to do anything else given their choice of timing for their deals, unaffected by any consideration of a Land Value Tax. There is nothing illegal about it, however much it inconveniences those who are merely trying to find somewhere to live.

A Free Lunch in 100 years?

Due to house price levels relative to incomes, it is reported that some lenders are offering 'inter-generational' mortgages. These loans, offered at higher than usual multiples of earnings, have such a long payback period that payment continues for life and children *inherit debt* in the form of an uncompleted mortgage. Maybe the grandchildren get the Free Lunch.

These loans are helping to bring new buyers who would otherwise stay away and bring about an earlier collapse of the housing 'pyramid', but at what cost?

100-year mortgages have been around in Japan for some time and are a factor behind the hugely speculative property boom that was part of the problem that caused the current 10-year recession. Brian Reading in his book (*Japan the coming collapse* Orion 1992) records that residential land prices multiplied by 200 times whilst wages rose by 21 times from 1955 to 1990. At the height of the boom 85% of tenants had abandoned ever being able to buy a home *even on a 100-year mortgage*. The Japanese government's Housing and Urban Development Corporation builds 25,000 houses a year for sale at cut-prices and *chooses the buyers by running lotteries!* These should be cautionary tales whenever we observe housing prices roaring ahead.

Construction volatility

The construction process is slow and building does not start until landholders release land. The planning process can only react to applications when made and permissions can only follow after due processes. These factors restrain supply which affects price rises at times of high demand. Volatility affects the industry in other ways. When the market crashes and work drops away, some workers and craftspeople leave, never to return, and it can be difficult to attract new recruits to such an unsteady career. As a boom gathers pace and new construction work absorbs labour, the maintenance and repair of existing buildings is affected adversely, whereas such work ideally requires steady attention. Clearly every industry has problems due to business cycles but few have the added difficulties of operating in such a monopolistic and volatile market as that of land.

Land Restoration, Nationalisation or Taxation?

Henry George pointed out that it was inappropriate to *restore* land to families in modern times. Equal land rights for all, in an industrial society, would be impractical and pointless.

Neither did he call for the *nationalisation* of land in the manner of Karl Marx and the socialists. George thought that the extension of government for such a thing was undesirable and, besides, the confiscation of private property would achieve nothing that the Land Value Tax could not do very simply alone.

Land Value Tax shares out the society-inspired *value* of land, but leaves ownership unaffected.

Wealth does not trickle down to the poor

Politicians have two main remedies for failure in our economic system which are dealt with in more detail in Chapter 6, but a little on them is helpful here.

Firstly, the hope is that wealth produced by a thriving economy will 'trickle down' to the poor. Over the decades the poor do achieve a gradual improvement in their living standard, but their *relative poverty* barely shifts, due to the way landed property (real estate), always attracts the increasing wealth and drives up this basic cost for everyone. Until this is addressed, poverty will remain with us and subsidised housing and much other welfare will be a major charge on the better off. Any 'trickle down' effect that might be working is massively counteracted by the way that the newly created wealth is attracted, like a magnet, into land wealth.

Heavy conventional taxes have not lightened the load for the poor

The second device that it is hoped will banish poverty is to redistribute wealth downwards by taxing those who create it. This method is counter-productive and could be regarded as a fine on a wealth creator like a penalty on a wrongdoer and besides, it is ineffecetive.

Henry George's four points about tax

George gave four fundamental conditions for a satisfactory tax regime:

- Firstly, that the tax should bear as lightly on production as possible

- Secondly that it should be easily and cheaply collected and fall as directly as possible on the ultimate payers
- Thirdly that it is certain to be paid and not evaded by falling prey to corrupt collection
- Fourthly that it bears equally so that no one is given advantage or put to disadvantage.

Some of our taxes work against production, some fail to be collected, some are particularly hard on the poor. They seem at times to work as a 'penalty' or a 'fine' for those who are productive and successful. For example, Value Added Tax raises the price of goods and services and this limits the amount of goods bought with a given amount of money, and it can be evaded by 'black economy' cash transactions. Income tax can deter people from taking work, and if labour is short this can force wages higher, making products and services more expensive. Tax on essentials, like petrol for example, needed by everyone, falls relatively more heavily on the poorer. Tax on capital can sometimes be avoided by sending the money offshore beyond the grasp of the Inland Revenue. Council Tax is levied by considering the house and land values together, so that if you improve your house by adding an extension, you not only pay VAT on all the goods and services used to build it, but after the next banding review you will pay more Council Tax when your house is placed into a higher tax band. This illustrates the negative effect of taxing production (the house extension). The owner has bought goods and given employment to architects, bankers, builders, brick makers, decorators, furnishers, etc., and the project will have increased the supply of good modern housing. All these are admirable things in any society. But the largest single financial beneficiary of such creativity is likely to be the Government which receives the tax paid on goods, services and employment. If Land Tax replaced these taxes, the owner could either have used money for other purposes or built a larger or better equipped extension, in the process creating more employment and reducing the number on welfare support - for which the taxes are currently needed.

Helping taxpayers to make money

Land Value Tax (LVT) would encourage the taxpayer to make money *through* the taxed land. It would encourage greater efficiency in the use of land and of the buildings on them, so that underused land and buildings in desirable locations would be released for development, which would save some green fields from building. In the case of the Centre Point building in London mentioned earlier, if the land value had been taxed the owners would have been given an incentive to let the building, providing much needed office space for businesses besides providing rent to pay the land value tax due.

This effect is additionally helped if some or all existing taxes were to gradually be replaced by LVT and similar taxes on other resources. Ideally and in the longer run VAT, income tax, capital gains tax, inheritance tax, Council Tax, etc, might be abolished. Freeholders would be liable for LVT only on the land value of their property. It would relate to the market determined value of the land alone as considered completely empty of any buildings or other works, but surrounded by its current local environment. This tax regime would *encourage* owners to carry out work which would be free of any tax, to help pay their LVT. They might build a bigger extension or self-contained flat to enable space to be rented out. LVT brings land into use which is 'underused' as defined by the planning policy, and this increased supply would force the land market to work more like a free market, moderating price rises or reducing them. As mentioned earlier, in Hong Kong, where the value of land funds government spending, all land is leased from the state. Hong Kong, until the recent handover was rated as the top economy of the free world in terms of consistent and actual growth; maybe their use of land values for the general good was the key. Tax on businesses were only levied on large enterprises. However there is no need to nationalise land to achieve the same benefits, since LVT leaves land privately owned.

Henry George's four conditions fulfilled
LVT as a single tax fulfils Henry George's conditions for a satisfactory tax regime.
- Firstly, it *encourages production,* as freeholders find ways of producing income to pay the tax. For example, new building works that could be rented to raise income for the tax or sold to pass on the liability.
- Secondly, concerning the *collection,* it relies on accurate land valuation which is the normal everyday work of valuers and surveyors.
- Thirdly, concerning *evasion and certainty of payment,* land is impossible to hide like some capital is. It could cut the need tax for tax planning services and make *'tax avoidance'* meaningless.

- LVT is impossible to evade since most owners can easily be traced.

- Fourthly LVT falls on the freeholder with very *little chance of being passed on to others* since, in competing amongst themselves for tenants, landlords would attract tenants with favourable terms rather than repel them with higher charges to cover the new LVT liability.

What do Helen Keller (1880-1968) and Albert Einstein (1879-1955) have in common?

They both believed that Land Value Tax should replace other taxes.
Others who thought the same:
Adam Smith (1723-1790)
John Stuart Mill (1806-1873)
Mark Twain (1835-1910)
Winston Churchill (1874-1965)
Milton Friedman (b.1912)
Henry George (1839-1897)
Leo Tolstoy (1828-1910)
Frank Lloyd Wright (1869-1959)
Franklin D Roosevelt (1882-1945)
David Lloyd George (1863-1945)

Many of the founders of socialism such as Bernard Shaw, Kier Hardie, amd Beatrice Webb were influenced by Henry George and his promotion of Land Value Tax, but they preferred other taxes, rejecting the idea that tax on land should be a priority. The legacy of their heavy taxation on human creativity and their bias for centralized economic direction are with us to this day. The nationalisation that they introduced was thought by Henry George to be undesirable and quite unnecessary.

The time is ripe for a reassessment of the ideas that Henry George was so influential in spreading before socialism was given its long experiment.

Beneficial spin-offs

The days of 'upward only rent reviews' for commercial tenants could be numbered as landlords scrambled to attract tenants. At the introduction of LVT more than the usual supply of building land would be released by those owners who found there was no one they could pass the tax on to. This would keep the lid on land price rises. Finally, LVT in place of other taxes would tax more fairly than current methods. At present the poorest cannot escape taxation on things they buy and if working, on their hard-earned income, whilst the Free Lunch gains of freeholders who see huge rises in their land values year on year, pay nothing on them. Reductions, and even abolition of the employment taxes of National Insurance and Income Tax, would encourage employment, reduce costs, lower prices and promote economic activity. For some businesses, the reduced overheads due to lower property costs would encourage marginally profitable ventures into life, thus helping employment. LVT, which taxed the land asset within the lifetime of the homeowner could, with some justice, be matched with the abolition of inheritance tax, especially on real property assets.

Land Value Tax in practice

An example from California in the early 1900's (mentioned by Harrison 1983: see Appendix C) tells of how a large area of underused farmland shared by less than a hundred farms became owned by over 7000 family farms because Land Value Tax was levied.

No nationalisation or reapportionment was made by government. The whole scenario was transformed as the original farmers made commercial decisions. The outcome was that thousands of intensively worked farms came in to being which could then support individual families.

The new farmers could improve their land knowing that any capital work to increase the yield from the land and help cover the land tax was excluded from the tax assessment, which only regarded the value of the land itself.

The pressing need for high-wealth individuals to hide it away in tax havens would reduce with the removal of conventional taxes. If in the ideal case, taxation was only imposed on land, oil, radio waves and other natural resources, and on society generated resources, there would be no reason for the existence of tax havens. Wealth would return home bringing its spending and investment benefits.

The gains to families, businesses and the economy through LVT are in contrast to the current system which forces those wanting to increase their production and wealth to leap the various hurdles of business rates, high rents and government inspired employment costs. For nearly a century we have had varying levels of largely socialistic experimentation aimed to help the poor, whose relative poverty has not shifted by discernible amounts over many years. Meanwhile governments carry out more and more tortuous tinkering with benefits and use counter-productive and often increasingly secretive taxes. It is surely time for the insights of the classical economists, Henry George and others to be given serious consideration so that our problems can be tackled with a changed mindset.

5

THE HAND IN THE GLOVE

(Planning and the Lottery Principle)

The Bouncer

The Free Lunch Restaurant serves Land Wealth to those who can persuade planners to grant permission to develop.

The planning system in terms of the allegory of Chapter 1, can be regarded as a bouncer controlling the entrance to the Free Lunch Restaurant.
Planning rations the quantity and quality of the Free Lunches from land values in accordance with political preferences and current demands.

The approval of the bouncer can give a huge boost to the personal wealth of those favoured. Someone selling a green field for new building can gain at least 200 times the agricultural value - an amazing Free Lunch from a remarkable Wealth Magnet!

Many people look on from outside and never get past the bouncer.
The entry price keeps rising beyond their income.

THIS CHAPTER NARROWS IT FOCUS into how urban and rural planning, Land Value Tax, the Citizen's Royalty and housing affordability might inter-relate to the benefit of many people.

Repossessed homes were a feature of the recession of the early 1990's. 250,000 families who had embarked on house purchase in the preceding booming years found themselves without a home and many of them had the additional burdens of property-induced debt and no income as the recession also deprived them of a job. There are currently about 800,000 empty houses. In a recent year there was a 40% price rise in some London property when wage inflation was about 3%. Housing is so expensive that one household in four cannot afford to buy their own home and 80,000 families live in bed and breakfast accommodation. There are a growing number of places where the people who run public services - the police, nurses and teachers - cannot afford to live.

It would be unfair to blame the planning system for all this failure, after all, who puts a bouncer at a restaurant door? The miserable outcomes listed in the last paragraph are linked to the control that the political system exerts *through* the planning system. The political 'hand' is hidden, like a hand is hidden within a glove. Adam Smith's mysterious 'invisible hand' of the market in other areas of economic life brings its hopefully benign effect for all, as everyone goes about their own business as they please. But the 'hand' that operates through the visible planning system has effects which specifically do *not* allow everyone to go about their business as they please and it achieves this through policies, laws and regulations. Outcomes of planning, whether by aim or default, are: high land prices; restraint on home ownership; wealth locked away for decades for freeholders, and losses and distress for those who are caught in the bursting of the regular property bubbles. The Lottery Principle is clearly operating despite the regulation of Land Use Planning.

Adam Smith's free markets are championed for their ability to supply goods and services when and where needed at reasonable prices. Choice is the key, as suppliers see what consumers want and fulfil the need. But how does such an idea work with land? Land Use Planning is an artificial restraint on the land market, which if removed would have several effects. Environmental quality would be lost, as inappropriate developments were juxtaposed, and the character of open countryside, with distinct towns and villages would be changed. Some services and facilities like schools and hospitals would become either too busy or slack as local populations climbed or fell. Some areas would become less crowded and the roads less busy. In general, the removal, or drastic easing, of planning rules would cause property prices to fall as everyone became able to develop more freely. High prices could still be commanded in sought-after areas, but the wide choice elsewhere would ease price rises and dampen their volatility. But land would still have a value and every plot its price, even if they would generally be lower than now.

The appearance and amenity of both country and town is of concern to most of us, but an effect of restrictive planning system is to keep land prices high and housing costs absorbing a large proportion of household income. But surely, good *planning* in any area of life involves the taking of steps to prevent surprises as far as possible. So why cannot the *'planning'* system achieve what the word implies – an orderly, foreseen supply of land at affordable prices?

Price volatility in any market is a result of a temporary shortage or over-supply. The planning and house-building process cannot respond instantly at times of high demand to make much difference to prices. Whatever rockets up fast, can also crash as demand drops and prices collapse.

At the time that Henry George was pointing out that general prosperity always raises land (and therefore housing) prices and take them beyond the reach of the poor, he was speaking before the highly restrictive Land Use Planning of today brought its own effects. This chapter discusses how Land Value Tax would interact with Land Use Planning.

Planning regulation grew out of concerns over public health following epidemics associated with unhealthy living conditions as industrialisation progressed. The early legislation covered the need for uncontaminated water supplies and the disposal of sewage; other regulations have followed such as those concerning light, ventilation, safety, structure, fire and electricity. The Mosaic regulations about the safety wall around a flat roof and about food hygiene and the safe disposal of sewage, were for the purpose of saving life and limb. But people died due to public health shortcomings associated with the Industrial Revolution simply because no one took the implications of these ancient regulations seriously enough. The pursuit of profit took a priority over the needs of a fairly expendable workforce. The health and safety aspects of our planning system could be said to be in keeping with the dictum: *'love your neighbour as yourself'*. But having ensured basic health and safety provision in housing matters, planning alone is not equipped to deal with the many dire problems that were listed at the start of this chapter.

The response of governments to problems housing affordability is to deal with symptoms and not root causes. These vary:

* Housing Benefit directly to individuals and families
* direct government grant to the Housing Corporation (a modern version of the earlier direct building of council-provided housing)
* demands to developers for quotas of affordable housing in their housing developments
* tariff charges on development
* whatever tinkering is deemed to be needed when politically embarrassing crises loom - such as the housing difficulties experienced by workers in 'key' public services such as nurses, the police and teachers.

The only device ignored in all this - a universal Land Value Tax - is the only one that will beneficially and permanently transform the situation.

The way our society allows some to gain through the ownership of such an essential thing as a home whilst at the same time excluding others, is highly divisive. The renters are losing two benefits: the security of having their own home and the financial gain usually associated with such ownership. The root problem is beyond anything that the planning system could possibly achieve and involves some matters that have already been investigated in earlier chapters and others yet to be mentioned. The remainder of this chapter investigates how planning would interact with Land Value Tax.

A. URBAN PLANNING -TOWN CRAMMING

The Mad Tea Party

In *Alice's Adventures in Wonderland*, by Lewis Caroll, at the Mad Tea Party, the following conversation took place:

> 'Have some wine' the March Hare said in an encouraging tone.
> Alice looked all round the table, but there was nothing on it but tea. 'I don't see any wine' she remarked.
> There isn't any' said the March Hare.
> 'It wasn't very civil of you to offer it' said Alice angrily.

A central plank of current government planning policy on towns known as Planning Policy Guidance Note 3 (PPG3) seems to be written with the same wishful thinking of the March Hare, that merely to coin pleasant soundbites like: **'more environmentally sustainable'**, will bring less noise, pollution and traffic, even though the policy detail of PPG3 - more people in towns and denser building - is likely to *increase* all these things. As the March Hare might have asked: 'Is the confusion intentional, or is it deliberate?

The planning system fails to achieve affordable housing for everyone who wants it; and the little it does achieve, is only through heavy bureaucratic intervention.

The current policy is to provide as much new housing as possible within existing urban areas. The urban policy is outlined in the Government's Urban White Paper (UWP) (November 2000) and the Planning Policy Guidance Note 3. (PPG3).

They can be seen on website: odpm.gov.uk (Crown Copyright).

Definitions:
Brownfield and Greenfield building

- A brownfield site is any site that has had development of any sort on it before. This could be a factory site or a railway yard, a house with a garden or several houses and their gardens taken together.

- A greenfield site is one that has not had development of any sort on it before.

The policy aim is to use brownfield sites in preference to greenfield sites. Thus for example, back gardens in leafy suburbs are more likely to be dug up and new houses packed in, in preference to new development on agricultural land at town edges.

To achieve a reduction in digging up green fields, the policy aim is to build houses in existing built up areas at a higher density than at present, that is: town cramming. The aims can be summarised:

> 'tackling the poor quality of life...and reducing the impact which urban living has on the environment'
> 'good design and planning which makes it practical to live in a **more environmentally sustainable** way with less noise, pollution and traffic congestion' (*emphasis as text*)
> 'to promote...a greener residential environment; greater emphasis on quality and designing places for people *(PPG 3)*

Along with these fine words it is startling to find that the most important recommendation is to build houses at higher density:

> 'Create a planning presumption against excessively low density urban development'
> 'avoid developments which make inefficient use of land...of less than 30 dwellings per hectare...encourage...more efficient use of land...between 30 and 50 dwellings per hectare' *(PPG3)*

But can the aim of *improving* towns ('less noise, pollution, traffic congestion...a greener residential environment') really be compatible with the high density solutions? More people means more traffic movements, whether public or private, causing more noise, congestion and pollution. Does the policy add up?

Over recent decades houses have usually been built to densities of 25 dwellings per hectare (11/acre) or less; but this density will no longer to be tolerated, instead, densities of up to double (50/ha), are to be encouraged, in some cases prescribed, and in some exceeded. To get an idea of the impact, walk around a housing estate built in the

1960's, '70's or '80's and picture what it would look like if double the number of dwellings were there, with double the cars and people. Even allowing for reducing household sizes overall, how are pressing environmental issues to be resolved when so many extra people are to be more densely packed together?

The policy to transform derelict or marginally profitable brownfield sites of factories into housing, makes good sense. But to use the full extent of these sites entirely for dense development will create another problem; that of denser urban traffic generated by the greater density of people. With the high density policy, it is much more difficult to create any natural environment, for example to replace parts of an old factory site with some open space and large trees. The doubled density of 50 dwellings per hectare, severely limits the amount of low rise, family-friendly houses with gardens and nearby green public spaces. It seems more logical for developments to be at *lower* densities overall if the requirement is to 'promote a greener residential environment'.

The desirability of houses in Georgian or Victorian squares is witness to the preference that people have for living in green surroundings. The new policy seems biased towards bleaker, not greener, town streets. If the number or total area of green features in a district remains constant but the population doubles, then the impact on the environment will double and the environmental amenity as experienced by the people living there will reduce. The policy cannot 'reduce the impact which urban living has on the environment' *in towns,* unless green features or areas *in towns* are at least *doubled.*

The Urban White Paper acknowledges that there is a flow of people away from urban areas:

> 'the challenge(s) we face include... encouraging people to remain in, and move back into, our major towns and cities, both to the benefit of our urban areas and to relieve the pressure for development in the countryside'

If town desertion is to be addressed realistically, town cramming seems a 'solution' that will achieve little. *People choose to leave towns for a variety of reasons, but if housing densities are increased will this make them want to come back? Will fewer leave?*

The Woodland Trust, commenting on the Urban White Paper, regretted that the need for trees and urban woods has 'been sidelined...ignored...scarcely acknowledged'. With such a bias towards high density urban house building, it is not surprising that more trees cannot seriously be considered in towns. Hillary Allison

(Policy Director, Woodland Trust), champions the need for greener towns and in November 2000 the Trust's website (woodland-trust.org.uk) reminded of the benefit derived from trees and wooded areas in towns, - turning brownfield sites into green fields - since they lead to improved air quality and bring human well-being.

A study in the United States has shown that there is a measurable therapeutic effect due to the proximity of foliage to people. Post-operative hospital stays were reduced for patients who were able to see trees and plants from their hospital wards, in contrast to the longer stays for those without such views. What is good for hospital patients must be good for the rest of us, even when we have no acute medical problems.

Some of those in favour of more dense urban areas quote that the density of other European towns is higher than towns in the UK and therefore we should follow suit. But even a superficial knowledge of, say, Paris reveals that the French incorporate balancing features in their more crowded housing that are absent from UK housing. Paris is more densely packed, but on an individual level in London we are either *in* the house or *outside*. By contrast, Parisian apartments, at whatever floor level, have at least one mini-balcony with a full height door or window, which opens onto the street space. This gives Parisians an enjoyment of outside conditions from the privacy of their own home. A benefit not often available to Londoners.

On the other hand London has parks of all sizes to which most people have free access. In Paris there are some beautiful lawns, but you cannot sit or lie down on them as Londoners are able to in the enormous fields that are the central London parks. This feature of town life in London has evolved from ancient times. As the city spread to encompass the villages, not all the countryside was allowed to disappear completely; it has now become the parks that are such a boon to London's amenities. In Paris such open spaces are further away from the centre. Long established patterns of lifestyle, culture and individual expectations are very different across national boundaries. To reduce the housing argument to: 'We must increase our housing densities to those of the French and the Spanish' is simplistic and concerns itself with one narrow measure of cultural and social life only.

Reality from a train window
A good way to assess the impact of Town and Country Planning on the broad scale is from the window of a train or car as one leaves the

centre of a large town on a cross country journey. The traveller proceeds and leaves densely packed development at the centre, through the lower-rise suburbs, and then the landscapes unfold, consisting of mile after mile of fields, woods, rivers, hills and forests with scarcely a sign of human habitation. For London, at about 15 miles from the historic centre, and for most of our county towns at under 2 miles, the empty fields start.

Yet there is a strongly held view that the countryside is under threat of being 'covered with concrete'. From the air everywhere looks empty and deserted. Under the highest estimates for development, the urban area for the South East outside London to the year 2016 will increase 1% only, bringing the total to 13%, and still leaving 87% rural.

A Forestry Commission study records that the south east is the most wooded region of England, and that woodland areas have grown by one third since the 1939-44 war. One problem for planners is the very size of the developments being put forward. Sites of hundreds of acres are too big to absorb easily in most localities especially given the NIMBY (Not In My Back Yard) attitudes engendered by the ugliness introduced by such tight cramming.

What might be more acceptable could be more, but smaller, developments introduced into communities more appropriately - at low densities. But the pressure on planners is such, that they have allowed large housing developments to encroach on to river flood plains and thousands of people were disrupted in the floods of the 2000/01 winter as a consequence.

Effects of cramped towns

The new urban high density policy means that in redevelopments and in new developments, two storey houses will be replaced by houses with three and four stories which cast longer shadows and cut out light. They will block the over-the-rooftops views of distant trees, a low skyline and clouds, and replace them with tall facades of brickwork and windows. Such neighbourhoods will become the norm as housing densities are doubled. Bungalows will become a rare breed.

Higher buildings will mean more homes utilising accommodation further from ground floor level (without same-level access to private garden space), and these are not helpful to families with young children. A family needs safe outside space for children to play freely whilst being easily monitored. A parent in a dwelling on a floor above ground level, either has to stay with their child outside themselves, precluding their own activity within their flat; or allow the child to play, possibly out of sight and beyond quick access in emergency. As the proportion of housing of the 'ground floor plus garden' type falls relative to the increasing supply of accommodation above ground floor, scarcity will drive up the price of the remaining family-friendly properties, to the detriment of all family budgets and especially of those of the poor.

High density housing brings privacy problems and unwitting intrusion even with the best of neighbours. The policy promotes tightly packed houses near major roads and motorways, within earshot of their continual drone of traffic that also pollutes the surrounding air. These developments are astounding. Would anyone even consider living in such a bad situation if they had a real choice of quieter, less crowded and less polluted situations? If anyone questions that *'love your neighbour as yourself'* should have relevance to Town and Country Planning, the development of housing areas close to such busy main transport routes, ought to convince them. The Urban White Paper positively encourages the development of housing near main transport links, but how close? What health safeguards are there to be? Country and Town policies are working together, using the unfounded fear of 'covering the countryside with concrete' to promote the 'burying of towns in brickwork'.

The case for towns

Towns are extremely convenient for their concentration of facilities and cultural activities, and as market places for all types of products and services. They expedite business generally in a materially successful society. Many enterprises and activities are only viable in a crowded town. Many of the most desirable towns are those which developed centuries before modern town planning was established. Such oddities as monumental architecture juxtaposed with the vernacular give a charm to town and cityscapes and reveal compromises which have grown up over centuries. The danger is that the new doubled density policy will suddenly impose developments without empathy. The policy is merely exchanging high density blots on the landscape for high density blots on the townscape.

The future of towns - gridlocked and greenless?

The high density policy is biased *against a new greening of towns* (where there is little green already), and *in favour of the preservation of green town edges and country* (where there are huge green areas).

This is a case of 'institutionalized selfishness' enshrined in government policy and planning law. A more favourable green policy would recognize that towns and town dwellers are experiencing a huge green deficit compared with country dwellers, and address this problem rather than increasing it with an urban high density policy. Instead of lamenting the fact that so many people are leaving, why not understand this trend and promote more green developments, *lower* the density on some brownfield sites below the maximum and make them attractive? The town desertion trend might slow or even reverse, given time. Policy makers are hoping that the town cramming policy will stem the spread of the urban areas into the countryside. But the inexorable increase in traffic, parking pressures and crowding associated with more people in the localities being redeveloped, is likely to encourage others to consider leaving town.

Objections to individual schemes are not, as yet, on the scale of town-edge protests. Urban renewal sites are usually relatively small and generally involve plots that contained buildings of some sort already. These could be such as the replacement of a short low terrace with a four storey apartment block, or building over back gardens. People living only three or four streets away from such developments may hardly be aware of them until they are occupied when it becomes harder to find car parking space in the streets. This lack of awareness of urban development limits the strength of opposition at the proposal stage. This is in contrast to greenfield proposals on town edges which cover huge sites of many empty acres and generate heated opposition because the development is so obvious to many people. The urban green lobby has, up to now, lost out to the edge-of-town green lobby.

Deregulation is generally achieving benefits of lower prices and more choice for consumers in many areas of life. But the planning system for land use, the last bastion of regulation, achieves no such things. Homebuyers accept price rises as a part of life and their choices become more restricted with each passing year. For example, as gardens are built on, so the choice of such less cramped plots is permanently reduced. It is highly doubtful that new public transport investment can ever hope to *improve* travel given the expected increase in the urban population desired by the Urban White Paper. Is choice in housing to be increasingly proscribed? Why should people in towns bear the whole brunt of new development which brings extra crowding, noise, pollution and travel problems? By opening up a little more countryside to appropriate development, it would make *little difference to the environment of the country,* but turn the tide of heavy environmental degradation in towns making them more pleasant to live in.

B. RURAL PLANNING – EMPTY LANDSCAPES

The Rural White Paper (RWP) (November 2000) states the case for the countryside:

> 'Living in the countryside has a great deal to offer. People value the quietness and sense of space, the beauty of the natural surroundings, the traditions and sense of community'

> 'Rural landscapes, green spaces, wildlife and the heritage features created by man's interaction with them lie at the heart of why people value the countryside so highly. They are a precious asset, providing enjoyment, refreshment of body and mind, cultural inspiration, opportunities for improved health and expanding potential for recreation.'

> 'more efficient use of urban land will help stem migration from towns to the countryside'

Country dwellers experience the demand on space around them caused by the migration of urban workers who arrive in search of improved living surroundings. This forces up house prices, leaving some country dwellers, or their children, priced out of the market. Villages are tending to become dormitories as the commuters desert the place from dawn until dusk. Bus routes are withdrawn, bank branches, shops and post offices are closed, rural railways went decades ago. Village life, which provided local work and a network of helpful relationships is a shadow of what it was, or could be if *more* people came and settled through a less restrictive planning policy.

Acres of bland empty fields, the product of centuries of human agricultural development and not 'naturally original' in any sense, are now set aside as surplus to agricultural needs, and their wide spaces lie largely unappreciated except by a few walkers. Farmers are subsidised to protect them from cheaper produce from poorer countries overseas, but cannot provide income for themselves through developing small portions of their land for the integrated development that rural communities need to maintain their viability. Yet their fields, unless permanently set aside, that is 'developed' in new ways, are of limited benefit in producing a greater diversity of wildlife.

The country has just those features that the town is so badly short of: space, a cleaner environment and the natural world. The picture is emerging of a growing imbalance between town and country and of policies that will exacerbate the differences.

Denunciations of rural development seem to be based on giving the preservation of the visual effect of the empty landscape a priority over every other consideration. Understandably, those who live on the edge of any human settlement, be it a sprawling conurbation, small town or a village, value the country view as much as those who enjoyed it before their own houses were built. Whereas the use of inner city derelict docklands to provide new, towns-within-towns is helpful in preserving some green fields, the abrupt arrival of huge cramped developments on the green fields that are to be developed, are too sudden and inappropriate for existing communities.

The high-density policy for those few large fields that are developed neither respects the need in the market for reasonably priced choices of dwelling and plot, nor the need to introduce new development in established communities in an orderly way with respect to them and their existing environment. Hence NIMBYism.

C. THE BATTLE OF THE EDGES

Clearly a planning 'free for all' is out of the question. However, the current attempt to cram development within existing town boundaries by redeveloping at high density, is likely to result in a growing protest from town dwellers. They will increasingly realize that their environment is threatened in order to maintain the pleasant surroundings that the people living in open country and at town and village edges now enjoy. To the traditional two areas of town and country could be added a third: 'town and village edges', to describe the sensitive area between urban and open country. This is where the controversy rages most fiercely. The edges of towns have traditionally grown outwards into green fields, and it is accepted that some green fields will still have to be built on. But now, these fields that will have to be used, are to be developed at double the usual density. Clearly, opposition about this from edge-dwellers will redouble with the density. As has been noted, high density building results in fewer choices of reasonable sized gardens with large trees and green spaces, which traditionally replaced such plots lost as the inner town was built up. Trees and general planting on generous sized plots at town edges help to blend the building with the country beyond, breaking up the harshness of stark buildings, and bland brickwork and roofs. But the new policy will result increasingly in dense masses of housing towering like tidal waves poised to flood the countryside with so little empathy for their setting in the landscape.

In the intense debate about green field development, urban densities, NIMBYism and so forth, it is helpful to grasp the contrast between the urban and rural densities. 'Crowded', 'open', 'cramped', 'empty' and such words are useful but they are subjective and some numbers are helpful. The contrasting densities of a county town and of the surrounding countryside can be grasped by the following example.

The Hampshire County Council report *A Profile of Hampshire* (July 2000) gives the density in the urban part of the Winchester District, as 29.5 persons per hectare; and in the rural part as 0.4 persons per hectare. (11.9 & 0.16 persons per acre). In the towns people share every acre of space with eleven other people. In the country (including its small towns and villages), they enjoy six acres all to themselves; *this is 74 times the space in the country, per person, compared with the town dweller!* These figures show the reason for the countryside experience: 'the quietness and sense of space, the beauty of the natural surroundings…'(RWP); and for the urban one: 'the poor quality of life'…'the challenge includes: reducing the impact which urban living has on the environment' (UWP).

Noise pollution is less of a problem in the country due, usually, to the greater distances; vehicle pollution usually dissipates quickly due to less sheltered conditions and dilutes with distance, and there are fewer vehicle movements and over a wider area. Some problems of life just do not happen between neighbours if the next house is 10 or even 2 metres away. The increasing preponderance of connected town dwellings under the new policy, will exacerbate such problems where more people will have neighbours immediately above, below, and through the wall of the same building.

The trend towards packed towns could be counter-balanced by generous sized plots at the edges, phased in such a way that no locality was swamped by new building. To plan for low density housing in this way would not only help provide a greater choice of family-friendly homes, but also soften the abrupt change from town to country. This would result in a more acceptable greening of the town and village edge developments, which is quite impossible otherwise. It would cope with the total need for housing in a more even-handed way than the current policy, bring choice and be environmentally sound.

How towns and villages grew

The growth of towns and villages before industrialisation began, was usually by the intensification of density at the centre and new low density development at the edges. This eased the urban area into the countryside slowly over many decades.

The economically and socially thriving centre demanded the more efficient use of land and buildings, so that gardens of town centre houses were built on for commercial use. At the town edge new houses on large plots gave families suitable places to live.

Low density development barely exists in planning policy now. High density housing, appropriate to demand in the busy centre is to be imposed all over town, right up to the town edge, and beyond it where greenfields still have to be developed.

A low density housing policy at town and village edges which gave good sized gardens, would increase the number and total area of environmentally rich habitats, in contrast to the bleak and empty fields that they would replace. The alternative of packed-in houses with tiny gardens, reduces bio-diversity and produces an abrupt and insensitive visual transition to the countryside.

D. LAND VALUE TAX AND PLANNING

As noted, Land Value Tax encourages development, and given demand for housing, would promote the intensification of building to the maximum density of the planning policy (Chapter 4). Thus, since it forces the land to be used more productively, as the policy makers desire, it is an ideal device for the purpose. This outcome is used by some to support LVT as a 'green' tax. However, in encouraging more development at every plot of ground designated for building the outcome *at that plot* is less green than before, for instance, if a small remaining green space such as a garden, or several gardens, are built on. LVT's green credentials, like the current planning policy, are only gained because more development at one plot can theoretically prevent the digging up of part of a greenfield elsewhere. It is thus *selectively green.* It could be argued that the loss of a small green space such as an existing back garden to build one new house in an urban area, is more crucial environmentally for the towns than for such developments on the edges of towns, or in the country. Certain green outcomes are indisputable with the clearing up of town eyesores such as derelict sites, in place of building on green sites elsewhere. Although not all green campaigners will welcome the raised levels of economic and building activity caused by LVT, the simplicity and effectiveness, even elegance, of the economics of LVT, would probably be acknowledged as very attractive by many people. But more specific green policies may be needed for towns to address the inconsistencies of PPG3 so that towns can be made more attractive at the same time, due to LVT's intensification effects.

If a plot had Planning Permission for, say, residential use it would be charged Land Value Tax according to its residential use value even if no house was built. An owner might use it to keep a pony, which is a truly green use but which yields no income. If they did not have sufficient income from other sources to pay the tax, they would have to make a commercial decision to develop the plot to bring in income to cover the tax, or sell it to someone who would do so. Under current law such a plot bears no taxation and there would be no pressure to build on it, beyond the personal choice of the owner. Meanwhile the landowner is sitting on a potentially valuable asset in an appreciating market. If such a plot under an LVT regime did not have building permission it would only be taxed at its agricultural value or at its value as measured by its last recorded sale price, if higher. Similarly anyone owning green fields without planning permission at a town or village edge would be faced with a LVT demand based on the price they paid for it. If only those purchases following the introduction of LVT counted for tax, then people who had earlier bought at inflated prices in the hope of planning gain would not be caught retrospectively.

The New Labour government floated the idea of Tariff Charges on development in order to capture profit for funding such things as affordable housing. (Green Paper: *Delivering a Fundamental Change December 2001*). It was rejected overwhelmingly during the consultation period, New Labour seems to have learnt nothing from Old Labour's failures in this area, (see p.91: ***How not to tax land***). Such attempts are a reminder that the introduction of a comprehensive Land Value Tax will need careful handling; but its simplicity compared with the previous inadequate failures should make the task of education and marketing easier. To link it to the payment of a Citizen's Royalty would be vital.

If the planning policy were to be (hypothetically) 'free for all' i.e. complete freedom to develop, then agricultural land would gain in value as any field became available for building. On the other hand, currently high value urban land would drop in value through falling demand. But total LVT yield would be set to achieve whatever the financial requirements and political possibilities were, whichever planning policy pertained (i.e. whether dispersal, concentration or variations in between).

Choices for town dwellers

Will town dwellers campaign against the growing crowding of towns and its increasing degradation; just as the town-edge dwellers do against the loss of nearby countryside to dense development? Or will they just desert the towns faster? Town dwellers living in the pleasanter urban areas might demand more conservation areas to prevent further cramming. Under a Land Value Tax scenario, if the number of such preserved areas increased, the subsequent raised prices would also raise the total LVT yield of that locality. It would leave the less desirable parts suffering greater crowding, moderate their price rises and lower the LVT amount per plot, at least relatively. The Citizen's Royalty paid in any particular locality could be partly funded by the local yield of Land Value Tax. This might make town cramming or any other major development more acceptable because of the cash compensation through the CR payment. The scenario might be as follows. Intrusive development could lead to a drop in the value of land nearby, thus the Land Value Tax charge would be lower for those who suffered the downgrading. In addition and for a period, a higher Citizen's Royalty could be paid to those so affected, funded by the new LVT raised by the new development. Such direct linking of tax and benefit is known as 'hypothecation'; (one penny on income tax to go directly to school budgets is another proposed example of this). To introduce LVT without a reduction in other taxes and hopefully also a locally modified Citizen's Royalty, would result in both town cramming as a policy and LVT as a new tax being strongly resisted. People are likely to object for two reasons: firstly that their quality of life is going to deteriorate; and secondly, that LVT is just another ruse of a Chancellor of the Exchequer hunting for revenue.

Under LVT given the current intensive development policy for towns, there would grow up a more permissive attitude towards development, favouring *permission* rather than *rejection*. A freeholder could argue that their right to develop in line with policy and to enable them to pay the tax due on their land, overrode the arguments used by planners to reject their scheme.

Back garden battles

As has been noted, NIMBYism as a consumer resistance movement to development has up to now been particularly strong around large town-edge proposals that would swamp adjoining neighbourhoods. This is forcing development onto town dwellers who are becoming aware that their neighbourhood might be threatened as back gardens succumb to the dense packing of houses rejected from town edges. The amenities and convenience of the existing communities that the residents want to preserve in both types of location have arisen over the last 50 years or so due to a steady building programme under familiar and constant densities. This brought in new families with young children to keep local schools viable, has enabled shops, restaurants and pubs to invest and thrive, and funded improvements for public amenities. The danger is, that in resisting new development, communities will become unbalanced as younger families are excluded by price. This will bring its own problems in the future, where the ageing community will have fewer younger people to run the services that will be increasingly needed.

What pace of growth?

There is a need, according to some planners for a provision of 200,000 new housing units per year, although the actual figure built currently is lower. As there are about 22m households already, this represents an increase of less than 1%; for example, 10 new houses/flats in a small town of 3000 people. To share the new housing growth in an even way would achieve development that was unnoticeable to most people. In place of a few large dense developments that are planned to contain hundreds of houses in limited locations in town-edge green fields, scattered, small, and low density schemes would receive less opposition due to the scale. Although some urban areas may be too crowded already to receive any growth, at many town edges, growth rates higher than 1%, achieved with *small low density* development, might be acceptable to the NIMBYs. A local, temporary, addition to the Royalty payment for areas affected by larger than average development, might help to make such building more acceptable. LVT would moderate price volatility and level, and even reduce new-build demand as empty dwellings were occupied. The choice of larger gardens could return.

Rural choices

New development in hamlets, farmyards, single isolated buildings or even in open country, could fulfil the need for those who wish to have more space than is usually available. Our current restrictive planning regulations and the cost of land do not encourage such developments.

Any demand for small communities such as for a multi-generational family, could be satisfied by personal planning permission specific to the type of group intending to live there. This permission could be in the manner of the restrictive permissions already available for dwellings for agricultural workers. The land value would be lower due to the lower demand for such special social reasons, and this would be beneficial to families and other small communities. Another rural case might be for the building of dwellings in woodland to house the people needed to manage the woods. The planning laws and regulations would become aligned more to the needs and choices of people rather than the requirement to preserve an empty landscape.

One aspect of LVT under the current high density policy could adversely affect the release of land for building. At present a landowner of agricultural land might apply for planning permission with no expectation of starting development for a while, but merely to test their chances. These owners might be deterred from applying as they would become liable for LVT on the higher value achieved on the grant of permission. The effect that LVT would have on releasing plots with permission already, would probably compensate for any such witholding. However, unintended consequences can affect the best laid schemes and if LVT were accompanied by a more permissive planning policy towards low density development this would help to ensure a sufficient supply of land for building.

Biodiversity

Research carried out by the Game Conservancy Trust at Loddington, Leics., has shown that by appropriate planting, conditions can be created so that a greater variety of wildlife can thrive. In the Loddington scheme (late 1990s), at a working farm the numbers of song thrushes increased over five years to levels not seen since the 1960s. Such planting could be linked to low density housing developments, so that biodiversity would be enhanced on land that is currently subject to the monoculture of current farming methods, even allowing for the 'loss' of some land due to building. Also there are opportunities for new settlements centred on new wildlife reserves and sanctuaries. The desirability of new development near existing nature reserves is not usually welcome, on the other hand to create new nature reserves along with sensitively designed new development could solve several problems. It would utilise excess farmland; provide new income from visitors; provide desirable places to live for those with interests in wildlife; add to the biodiversity of the area, and help to compensate for the loss of habitat caused by major civil works such as airport and dock extensions elsewhere.

Bland fields enhanced. Rural communities strengthened

Current planning policy for the countryside is summarised in the policy note PPG 7:

> The guiding principle in the countryside is that development should both benefit economic activity and maintain or enhance the environment. Rural areas can accommodate many forms of development without detriment, if the location and design of development is handled with sensitivity. New development should be sensitively related to existing settlement patterns and to historic, wildlife and landscape resources.

Villages and small towns would be enhanced economically and socially through more variation in housing density within the policy. Examples of imaginative housing developments in the countryside and at town-edges include the development of large ex-hospital sites; converted stable blocks around courtyards; the conversion of large country houses into apartments; and such new high density developments as the Poundbury 'village' in Dorset. But few developments incorporate generously sized and readily extendable houses to accommodate larger (perhaps extended) family units than the ubiquitous '2 adults and 2 kids'. The price of land and the planning policy precludes such possibilities except for properties at the top of the range. Lower densities could encourage multi-generational living, family care of the elderly and the siting of small unobtrusive businesses within generously sized residential plots.

Two things that offend concerning the setting of the standard high density housing development (over and above the loss of a green field) are: the dreary duplication of building types, and the inability of the development to be blended and softened with trees because of the closeness of the houses.

It is recognised, within planning rules that a single monumental new building, can *enhance* a landscape, despite the loss of the green field, and some permissions have been granted for just such modern mansions, located in green fields away from any previous residential designation. But why would not a *whole new hamlet* similarly enhance a landscape, just as an ancient village does already? LVT, in lowering land prices would enable more of a development budget to be spent on the design, fabric (including energy conservation) and landscaping. Existing villages and hamlets that have been there since living memory are accepted just because they have been there for so long.

They do not inevitably sit starkly in their setting, they *are* and *make*, a new human setting. They have been blended in with the surroundings through the years as trees have grown up around them and the whole setting creates its own unique appeal. The planting and the general landscape eventually *absorbs* the built environment if plain, or *enhances* it if attractive, and even in newly designed hamlets and settlements the art of the landscape architect can achieve the matured look very early on.

The slow organic evolution of hamlets, villages and towns, with additions and adaptations evolving at a measured pace as often happened historically, would be more acceptable to the sudden infilling of a few huge vacant tracts of land on town edges.

The paradox of 'more is less'

The debate about rural development should include the paradox that in terms of visual intrusion, general amenity and environmental diversity, the use of more space in the countryside for the same number of dwellings could result in less visual and environmental impact. This is because of the increased amenity deriving from more diverse planting, the use of water and perhaps new common land. Impact is much reduced and softened with low density development containing planting as a screen. Low density could range from 3 to 5 dwellings per acre (7 to 11/hectare) down to 1 per acre (2/ha) or less.

To introduce low density housing at town edges in place of the proposed dense building would still leave most of the countryside untouched whilst reducing the need for some dense urban development. Small sensitively designed schemes in the countryside could provide a supply of desirable homes around settlements and villages on large plots.

A more permissive planning policy allowing some development of green fields at low densities, would ease the plight of farmers who could sell land, and not merely to raise the fairly low amounts of Land Value Tax they would be liable for. Farming and rural areas generally need solutions that will provide long-term alternative sources of income, and land sales would help bring a new income stream for many people. The reforms of this book form an integrated whole to meet some of the needs of people wherever they live, be it in towns or in the country.

The earth yields food with ever increasing effectiveness and it is accepted that the planet can feed more people than the forecasters of population tell us to expect, as long as distribution permits. Low density housing would satisfy a desire that an increasing number of people have for home-grown organic food and thus low density development would retain some ex-farming land for food cultivation. Here is another reason to encourage an idea that gives more choice for small scale enterprise and the self-sufficient way of life, which is otherwise becoming less available. Following the farming crises of recent times and the possible problems of genetically modified crops, many people might prefer to grow more of their own food.

Utilities

The provision of piped water, gas, electricity, etc, to the scattered dwellings of a low density scheme generally, is more expensive per dwelling, than for denser development. Pipes and cables runs are longer and thus need more work per dwelling to set in place. But options for locally based energy generation and storage are always increasing through improved technology and can even bring greener solutions than conventional sources, through the elimination of transmission losses. The use of wires for telephones is less necessary as mobile systems become more sophisticated. For water supply, boreholes are suitable in some places, and rainwater collection tanks with tanker supplies elsewhere. Given the increased space around low density housing, and appropriate ground conditions, sewage in remote areas is handled through septic tank arrangements, small treatment plants, suitably designed outfalls and appropriate vegetation. Rainwater runoff from houses and roads is more easily contained within a low density development. Rain thus absorbed by the land near where it falls, takes longer to travel to the streams and rivers than if taken immediately there by artificial drainage, as it may have to be from all the non-absorbent surfaces of high density development. Thus a low density option would save the cost of drainage and reduce flooding risks lower down the valley. Also, the greater planting possible around low density development absorbs rainfall, again reducing the net run-off.

The provision of utilities thus brings no insurmountable problems for low density housing development than for any other type. Any greater costs for these would be offset by cheaper land through the greater supply, achieved through Land Value Tax and, or, a more permissive planning policy.

Travel

A valued benefit of modern life is personal mobility, but it comes with drawbacks given that for historical reasons dwellings had to be located near workplaces. Since a particular geographic location is less important for many industries, some can be located almost anywhere given electronic communications. The active promotion of the dispersal of workplaces nearer to homes, or at home, would have many beneficial effects including the saving of wasted time in travel and pollution. Unfortunately the building of high density homes with the pressure on space in them and around them due to policy and high land costs, hinders rather than promotes this dispersal.

Given a policy of more dispersal, travel would increase in country areas, but the number of journeys would remain low in comparison to urban volumes, so rural pollution, whilst rising slightly, would not be to the harmful levels of urban areas, which is likely to increase steadily if the high density policy continues.

The failure to match the planning policy for transport with the planning policy for housing and business may not be physically, financially or politically solvable. There are many diametrically opposed policies involved. Given the continuing travel demand to ever denser towns it is difficult to see travel improvements bringing any real benefit beyond a short period following their completion. Rather than just dealing with the travel symptoms of inadequate planning, a new look at the policies themselves is needed. Current planning policy leading to the concentration and intensification of development in urban areas will also intensify travel problems there, whereas a policy of dispersal of both housing and business would reduce them.

E. THE ESSENTIAL PACAKAGE

Land Value Tax with the Citizens Royalty
A new tax that would especially affect the majority of voters who are freeholders would have to be introduced with care. The introduction of the Citizen's Royalty would ease the introduction of LVT because of its clear funding role for the Royalty. To have the benefit of a head start for the Royalty through banking reform contributions (Chapter 3) would make the idea attractive. A planning policy that promoted high density building linked to a locally increased Royalty for those affected could make such development more acceptable. The aim of the tax reform would have to be a net improved income position after tax for the poorest and with a majority of the rest being at least no worse off. It would be essential that some of the yield from

LVT should cover a reduction in conventional taxes, as well as part-funding the Citizen's Royalty (see Chapter 7). In the interest of bringing more security to the poorer and more choice to all, it is important that the ability that LVT has to redress the Free Lunch imbalance must be carried out *directly* in the form of regular income to each citizen. There have been too many false starts, in the bungled attempts associated with taxing land development to risk anything less than something like the rounded approach of this book. The Poll Tax (Community Charge) demanded tax irrespective of income or any chance of producing income to pay it. The introduction of LVT with the Citizen's Royalty would cover the LVT charge for many and net extra income for the poorest. Taxation is never welcomed. To merely promise a more elegant and fair system of taxation will never have the appeal to voters that the cash of the Royalty would have.

Land Value Tax should be phased-in with the Citizen's Royalty (raising the LVT rate of tax and increasing the CR payment over some time), whilst reducing or eliminating other taxes. This would demonstrate how the new taxes were affecting people and the economy generally and allow time for adjustment. (Appendix B).

How not to tax land

Various attempts by UK governments over the last half century to tax land values for public benefit are summarised in *Essays in Land Economics* (see Appendix C). They were named Development Land Tax and Betterment Levy.

They concentrated on active 'development' as builders and developers produced new homes and buildings. They muddled land values, which are the only concern of Land Value Taxation, with construction and building costs. They were complex pieces of legislation containing many anomalies and producing unintended results.

The legislation had a reverse effect on the supply of land to that intended. It made some developers hang back, leaving their land undeveloped beyond the reach of the taxman. They hoped that a new government would change the high tax rates or abolish the bad legislation, which always happened. Fewer houses were built. The political stunt of catching developers at the point of taking their profits misses the point that every homeowner is sitting on increasing value in their land as the housing market rises, as the increasing trend of mortgage refinancing and equity release bears witness to.

These Acts involving tax on the *new development* on land failed to grasp the principles of land economics that the classical economists defined over two hundred years ago, they ignored the experience gained on the working of LVT in countries on five continents since the early 1900's.

Valuations for Land Value Tax

A valuation of all land would precede the introduction of Land Value Tax. There have been several LVT schemes established over some years internationally to show that such a valuation presents no insurmountable problems. Denmark values land annually for LVT purposes at a cost including collection, of less than 2% of the yield; Johannesburg has experience of imposing LVT since 1919; Hong Kong has used land values to fund necessary public spending for well over a century. As an alternative to official valuation, to speed introduction, valuation might be the owner's own assessment. Self-assessment could be officially reassessed later and any tax adjustment backdated. One condition concerning self-assessment elsewhere has been that whatever the price assessed by the owner would be the price paid for the land if the government were to purchase the property, which would encourage accuracy. The imminent introduction of the tax would bring empty dwellings and other buildings back into use and improve the housing supply situation. Development already permitted would be brought forward as owners needed to find new tenancies to cover the LVT payments, or pass it on to new owners through a sale. Agricultural land would bear little LVT due to its low value. Agricultural land bought speculatively for possible housing or industrial use, but without Planning Permission, would be assessed on the purchase price as recorded at the Land Registry. Speculation in land would moderate and this would help to stabilise prices, since the buyer would be liable for a high Land Value Tax charge based on transaction price without a certainty that Planning Permission would be granted. Land prices would ease, and this, together with the arrival of underused buildings onto the market as mentioned above, would tend to lower the price of land with a reduction in costs for all house buyers.

Where now?

The scandal of the empty homes, the numbers of homeless and the increasing inability of the system to deliver a reasonable choice of house types for anyone earning an average salary, indicates a pressing need for different answers to those given by our system as it is. There is a substantial minority of people who are being left behind by not being freeholders, and many of those who are, do not really gain much. The Royalty with Land Value Tax and banking reform, would achieve more fairness in society and bring less distortion to the economy than conventional taxes do. Reformers need to be aware that the high density housing policy is likely to come under increasing opposition as people see what it is doing to their neighbourhoods. LVT, which would work to promote whatever maximum density the policy allows, might become unpopular by association, unless accompanied by the Royalty. This leads to the view that a *low density* policy should be added to the options available to planners for the many reasons already mentioned, but particularly to widen citizen's choice. The solutions this chapter gives are democratically empowering, realistic, financially possible and arguably 'greener' overall (for both urban and rural situations taken together) than the current town cramming/empty landscape policies. The full scope of these and other changes which cover a broader spectrum than planning, are summarized in chapter 7.

6

IS THERE ANY PLOT ?
(How democracies struggle with the Lottery Principle)

TWO QUESTIONS are being asked by the above title. The first is about the type of plot familiar in a play. In a good play there is an internal integrity and logic which the observer can appreciate from their own human experience, as the playwright unfolds the drama with characters and events interacting. The question for us here is: how successful and how mutually consistent are the devices used by those who try, and have tried over the years, to rectify the imbalances in our society that are thrown up by the tendency for the Lottery Principle to hold sway? The second question relates to the possible existence of the type of plot in life or fiction whereby some try and maintain their advantage through manipulation. The previous chapter dealt with this type of plot as it relates to the politics behind planning. This chapter brings other areas of life under scrutiny.

A. FAVOURING THE FAVOURED

J.M.KEYNES, one of the most influential economists of the twentieth century, recognised the unfairness of the society of his day, pointing out its inability to provide employment for all or a fair distribution of resources.

Now, many decades later, poverty and unemployment are still with us and the cost of welfare is burdensome. In the decade of the 1980's whereas average household incomes rose in real terms over one third, the bottom tenth experienced a slight decrease. Even a Labour government did not manage to reduce the number of families living in poverty. In the year 1999/2000 the same proportion of people (one quarter of the population) lived on less than half the average income as did three years earlier and the number of pensioners living in poverty remained the same, at 2.6 million.

If in *prosperous times a rapidly improving outlook* cannot be provide for those on low incomes then surely something is wrong and our economic system is failing us? But, as we have seen, the trend of continuing poverty would not have surprised Henry George who said that *poverty will always be associated with progress* for as long as we allow the wealth in land values to be taken privately rather than be shared by everyone. His point has been increasingly proved ever since.

As noted, it was Adam Smith who 100 years before Henry George, advised governments to treat the value of land as 'a peculiarly suitable source of public revenue'. But, although several nations and cities have done this in measure, in the UK no government has been able to grasp successfully the potential of Land Value Tax. Every economist knows of the advantages of using land values and the wealth of natural resources as a prime source of taxation. The absence of even a discussion on these well attested and intriguing solutions in the face of so many problems, is baffling and a motivation for this book.

Game playing

Imagine a tennis match where the court size for one player was different to that for the other. Or a game of football which ran on for one side without a break whilst the other team was able to send on any number of substitutes. Or where after every goal scored by the winning side the centre-line was moved nearer to it! Thankfully for games, this is the stuff of nightmares, but some aspects of everyday existence are like this for many people.

For a good game, players should be evenly matched and rules observed. Players relish the chance to prove themselves against many different teams so that it can be seen that they truly are the greatest, against all comers and under conditions of fair play. Good sport arises when the difference between the winners and losers is marginal. Large imbalances in performance between competitors are pathetic and embarrassing. Apart from the eventual champions, the ultimate triumph of every game must be that people show once again their ability to agree to fair arrangements, where winners are rewarded and that losers can re-enter the contest another day. Often this is without any financial gain as champions are acclaimed merely by recognition, and where the also-rans experience no loss, apart from pride.

However, in real life economics, winners accumulate the assets that are vital to independent survival for everyone, whilst countless others lose out, or merely hold steady at whatever they started with. Games fulfil a desire to see excellence rewarded in an atmosphere of fair play and Moses' arrangements helped towards that in the real world of economics in particular, and for society in general. They allowed for merit to be rewarded as the system ran on, but the regular restorative features interrupted the acquisitive tendency of the able, and ensured that the less competent were given another chance to survive independently. Whilst some people in our society enjoy 'fat cat' salaries of enormous size which should enable them to live materially secure lives into the future, many others exist just above the breadline with barely an asset to their name.

That an economic system might have game-like characteristics might seem a bizarre fantasy, but as noted, the running of the Mosaic socio-economic system bears striking similarities to the way that we play games. However, the similarity breaks down in one aspect. The celebrations at the outcome of a game are enjoyed mostly by the winners, but in that system, the celebratory features of the regular recreational and restorative intervals, were enjoyed most by *the losers.* During these events, they not only knew that others were not working to gain advantage over them, but that following the rest and celebration period they were enabled to start independently again. Moses' amazing system added hope to mere survival and was even fun! Even if times were hard for some, the reality was that the time was drawing ever closer when a reversal of circumstances would transform life for them.

Our governments deal ad-hoc with the problems of an increasingly unfettered capitalism. Complex tax rules arise to fund basic welfare for the losers. There are few schemes that encourage enterprise at the level of the individual which would enable the poor to become independent in the Mosaic manner. At the other end of the wealth spectrum great creativity and expense goes into the negative procedure of avoiding tax obligations. The game our society currently plays, has its rules changed frequently as the government tries to rebalance the needs and contribution of weak players against the contribution and ambitions of the strong. A delicate balance is attempted, or an uneasy truce kept, rather than a step forward for everyone together in an exciting game, where all might be empowered to be creative and entrepreneurial, whilst securing the basic needs of the weak. The challenge is to learn from Moses' high aims and everyday practicalities, and apply the principles to our technically more sophisticated but economically and socially more primitive times.

Game Rules

Game players start their games equipped equally, whether it be with suitable clothing or implements - imagine a game of hockey where some where playing without sticks! Rules for games make the boundaries for the players, and separate the game from the everyday world. The participants usually compete according to matched ability (e.g. related to age); the apparatus used in a game is chosen to test a particular skill, intellectual or physical, at a particular location; time limits are sometimes set overall and within the game; and there are specific instructions on how to start and progress, with explanations as to what constitutes unacceptable behaviour.

In the modern economy the privilege of being a fully participating player is open to very few people. Most of us are acting out a servant role (as employees) with little chance to change that way of life and become creative and self-reliant on our own account. Timing is a vital factor of many games and always has some relevance even if just for rest. But the real life economy runs randomly; a boom develops then falters quite unplanned and to the detriment of all, especially the poorest. We do not have ways of redress imbalances that grow up so that Free Lunches are restored to all. To some today, to introduce restrictions might be thought anathema in the current free and open market philosophy. But the model of Chapter 2 with its rules and principles did not restrict freedom overall, rather they *release more people to greater freedom.* This was achieved through the safeguarding of rights, the promotion of enterprise and the encouragement of good community and human relationships. These are based on the way people normally behave co-operatively when they are functioning as a team or as a focussed group with a common aim. The rules are not strange and foreign but they align with fair and familiar patterns of everyday life that link, rather than isolate people. If our wisdom never rises higher than the self-centred and acquisitive ideology fostered by increasingly capitalistic trends, then our society will fragment rather than cohere. Tensions build from these divisions, as the poor continue powerless and the vast majority, merely survive, with little security against global commercial forces.

These principles and rules are quite different to the failed and fading socialistic collectivism and its controlling tendencies. But merely to curtail them would just help to extend conventional capitalistic influences, leaving the poor less protected. New principles are needed as a replacement, since the Lottery Principle will always operate and needs purposeful countering.

Size matters: Large lame ducks vs. Small growing fledglings

The modern economy is increasingly global and funds move from country to country to maximise shareholder return through lower labour costs, taxation and risk. Governments have an interest in treating businesses favourably and attracting new ones in order to protect the jobs and livelihoods of their voters, thus grants and tax breaks are offered to help in difficult conditions. Large organizations, are able to afford the personnel to apply for these inducements and able to spend the time lobbying the government. They also have large numbers of workers, each with a vote, so they attract an understandable bias by attentive politicians. They are thus much more likely than small businesses to receive state help to keep afloat.

In 1999 the Corus steel plant in South Wales announced a drastic production curtailment. The government offered to pay half the wage bill for a year for 6000 people and to train them for other skills. The largesse is readily to hand when so many votes are at stake, and the effort and time for bureaucrats overseeing this hand-out would be far less than needed to divide the same amount of money between 6000 separate entrepreneurs in an attempt to establish new small businesses. Media headlines are more effective from such large deals and results are needed fast in politics. To those with a socialist mindset, the temptation to engineer employment solutions at a stroke by pandering to large corporations, must be very gratifying. Today if a small business survives and thrives, it is some achievement. But a fraction of the amount offered to Corus but spread among small businesses in the form of grants or better allowances would be far more effective in wealth production, as such work by the Prince's Trust shows. The targeting of the small businesses would need more manpower and time and would produce nothing in headlines, and so the political urgency to help is low. How newsworthy would it be to help someone into self-employment: such as to start selling healthcare products, develop as an artist, or start up as a car mechanic? Large lame ducks are more newsworthy than small lively fledglings.

Unusually, Corus refused to take the help. Such failing businesses normally rush for the cash and try to enlarge the handout, as did Lord Simpson when he sited Marconi's new research centre in Britain, to tap a £25m grant available from a fund of nearly £130m set up by the New Labour government in the late 1990's to help the Midlands following problems at Rover. Moses' system recognised that failure happens, but the bias was set towards the preservation of the small and against unfair accumulation by the powerful. The tools were economic but the motive was, far more importantly, political. There was to be no central government which by comparison to most other groups would have been very powerful. There was an evenness about the land holdings so that there was to be no build-up of unduly large private (family) holdings which could threaten the basic survival assets of families whose holdings were might have been taken in the process.

Corporations: When is an employee a slave?
A US study showed that the performance from investing every year in the corporation who paid their Chief Executive Officer the largest amount would have been abysmal. $10,000 invested in 1993 and reinvested in each year's 'pay leader' would have dwindled to $3585 by 1999, whereas the investment in the 'S&P 500' top 500 companies evenly would have grown to $32,301. The wealth-creating abilities of large corporations and their highly rewarded leaders is not always what is imagined.

The large modern business organization owned by shareholders who are not employees is a product of centuries of economic development that has paid no attention to the idea that every family should have the ownership of assets to provide for their survival and to empower them. Work for an employer as a medium term solution is useful to help out the temporarily poor. But the idea of a modern, remotely owned corporation employing large numbers of people, who see employment as their lifetime status and who have no ownership interest, is more akin to a slave enterprise of Moses' time. Samuel the judge, who was a leader after some centuries of the working of the Mosaic way had strong words to say about the pitfalls of this type of organization when he introduced the monarchy. Which institution bears a strong resemblance to the modern corporation with a remote power centre and essential hierarchy.

Limited liability: categorising people
The limited liability device, used for more than a century to promote technological and material progress, has increased the flow of capital needed in the process. Those with capital can invest in a new venture and yet protect their other assets in the event of failure. Limited liability also warns others who might deal with such an entity that they should be wary and this warning stems from the way the limited

liability concept can be used to avoid the obligations of relationship that Moses expected people to honour. The limited liability company encourages the separation of people from each other into categories of owner (shareholder), employer and employee. These categories are possible within Moses' system but the case of employment of one Israelite by another was to be temporary, with warnings about abusing the changed status.

The limited liability concept grew up out of the idea a distinct corporate entity such as a monastic order having a legal existence defined separately from the individuals who comprised it. Limited liability also arose to protect those people, for example, involved in civic affairs, from being personally liable if the town went bankrupt. The growth of world exploration and technology led to Governments granting charters to a group of individuals which was empowered to trade on its own account. This sharing of power due to the possibilities of commerce was to mutual benefit. The coming together of these corporations and limited liability meant that enterprises of greater risk (and maybe reward) were more likely to proceed.

The prime beneficiaries of limited liability companies are the shareholders who whilst trading for profit do not have to give as much consideration to other people's rights as without the device. The capital that they use, which in many cases historically grew out of the wealth based in the accumulation of land, is somewhat protected. The limited liability concept is still used to absolve the owners or directors of a firm from personal responsibility for such an important thing as health and safety, in contrast for example, to the clear personal responsibility that was expected in case of the roof safety wall of Moses' regulation. At its worst, limited liability can encourage reckless disregard for the assets and safety of others. But over the years, steady reform has ensured that responsibilities towards employees, consumers and the environment have to be considered even by limited liability companies. Religious societies, trade unions, consumer rights and environmental groups, among others, have campaigned against the indifference to the social consequences of activity which follows unfettered enterprise using the limited liability device. Broadly speaking these various welfare organizations are attempting to redress the balance in favour of the poorer, the disadvantaged and the environment. Had some of the laws of Moses and the general principles of the Law been specifically guiding the lawmakers in our business and economic life, the problems arising from changing technology and employment patterns, capitalism, etc., would have been countered earlier.

Some owners took these enlightened measures before they were obliged to by law. But limited liability is not a perfect protector and will not usually protect the smaller holders of assets against the claims of larger holders. These larger capitalists will protect their assets before entering into agreement with the smaller capitalists. For example, a bank lending to a small limited liability company, may require the directors to personally guarantee the loan, ascertaining first that the directors have assets such as a family home to cover possible failure. Thus does limited liability protect the interests of the more powerful against those of the less powerful. This is exactly opposite to Mosaic principles where it was the weaker who held the 'limited liability' advantage (for their debts) and the holders of spare assets who had responsibilities that they were not to avoid, for example to supply interest-free loans with the possibility of non-repayment.

Can liquidation, used by the shareholders of a failed company to limit their obligations be seen as a device similar to that of the seven yearly cancellation of the debts of the Mosaic poor? This might be true in some cases, as, for example, it can theoretically protect a family home from seizure if creditors have not used it as collateral. Thus could limited liability be seen as a device of a Mosaic type but only if applied to those who are protecting their most basic assets. But for those with more assets than this minimum, the protection afforded by limited liability is not of the Mosaic paradigm. It can be a kind of insurance for a rich debtor, against the interests of poorer creditors.

Under Mosaic law the poor could become slaves (employees) to Hebrews or foreigners to cover for their debts, but only for a limited period. There is a safety-net aspect of this use of temporary 'slavery' in that it enabled the poor to survive, but it never went beyond the release year - a maximum of six years. If they were enslaved to a foreigner, relatives were encouraged to release them sooner than this, with a payment. If they were servants to Hebrew masters, their liability for any outstanding debt ceased at the slave release year, which is a similar mechanism to bankruptcy in modern times. Those making use of our limited liability laws can sometimes avoid their moral if not actual obligations to creditors and return to business under another corporate entity. Under Moses there was an obligation to pay the debt, and the prospect of a family member becoming a servant or slave because of debt would, hopefully, prompt a family member to help if they could. There was no legal obligation for a family member to help out, but hopefully the family relationship would have been more important than the financial loss that the relative might have to stand. Clearly, personal relationships always play an important part in oiling the wheels of business, as obligations and responsibilities often work out to benefit of those who are helpful in their business dealings, whether blood-related or not. A difference today regarding personal failure in business, is that whereas a bankrupt person starts again at a *zero-asset* position; the Israelite citizen would return to a *full asset* position on their own land, when it was redeemed by a relative or themselves, or free at the 50th (jubilee) year.

Limited liability releases capital for the progress of industry, especially for those schemes that might be marginally profitable or risky. It is clearly a useful device to facilitate economic expansion whilst protecting wealth. But in the light of Mosaic principles, to protect wealth by avoiding obligations to the poor is divisive. It would be *favourable to the already favoured*, and limit the losses of the rich as a priority; which is quite the opposite way to the Mosaic way which was *favourable to the less favoured* specifically limiting the losses of the poor as a priority. That culture was one of enterprise with activity focussed in time-limited episodes; the successful were encouraged in their success, it was possible for all to have the opportunity to be successful, but for those temporarily poor not to lose hope. Whatever the advantages of limited liability, it can often work against the poorer and give security to the richer.

Too many spectators
There is no 'Free Lunch for all' in our society, as there was to be in the Mosaic one, based on land holding for all. Whatever other devices there may be for wealth creation, the 'Free Lunch for all' of personal workable assets, the most important, is omitted. The burden of supporting those who are never likely to get near a Free Lunch is getting so large that it is time to look at this feature of economics and bring the poor into the economy as fully participating players instead of bystanders. In our society, although self-employment does not necessarily need extensive assets in some areas of work, few have the inclination, or are prepared to accept the challenge, to be anything other than an employee. In our capitalistic system employers provide their workforces with 'just enough' income for their existence. Increasing education and advancing technology, with its need for skilled workers, and union action and universal suffrage, have all helped raise worker's income, and therefore improved their lifestyles over time. The welfare state has arisen in an attempt to

resolve capitalism's fundamental weakness, but it leaves many at the mercy of market forces. The much vaunted freedoms of the market play against the freedom of the poorer in society. The powerful will use the lack of restrictions in free markets to extend their power, and as always the poorer will become more oppressed, unless there are positive safeguards for them.

Mosaic principles clearly show that restriction and discipline is necessary in any society that intends to extend human rights to every citizen. The market had its place but basic human economic rights were a priority over an absolutely free market. Land ownership removed agricultural land and the site for the main residence out of the market altogether. The people would have had a lot less uncertainty about their future than the majority of us have. Town houses in his system were subject to a free market but that would not have affected the right of the ordinary family to live and survive on their own land. The case for town houses illustrates that the accumulation of wealth for any family was proscribed in law by a prohibition on holding other people's family land beyond the paid redemption of it, or beyond the Jubilee year. For us this difference between town or country residence is irrelevant whereas only the country house in the pastoral society was relevant for survival. The cycles for business activity, debt, land restoration and freedom from employment were clear and unequivocal. You knew exactly where you were; everyone knew. Certain behaviour was not permitted, you could not do a 'wonderful deal' in land if it meant that a family was turned off their land forever; the law prevented it.

The law upheld the dignity of everyone as equally important in the society, having the same rights and privileges as everyone else. Land rights were the basis of the certainty for the future of all the people. Compared with us, this gave great freedom and independence. Interdependency and co-operation benefited the whole nation as it prospered for hundreds of years without central government about 3000 years ago. We cope with poverty in our society by giving the right to a minimum income until the poor can become gainfully employed again. Moses' system of basic assets for all, must have ensured that very few regularly needed income support. The Citizen's Royalty would be the starting point to empower all in an equivalent way, with the poorest benefiting most.

Multiple rights (and one major responsibility)
Security brings confidence about the future. The panoply of rights

under Mosaic law, gave people a security about many things: land for housing and for survival through farming; return to their land if circumstances meant that they lost it due to poverty; debt forgiveness every seventh year; self-determination and a variety of options for survival in good times and bad, all backed by laws and without interference from any central government; that others would help out if misfortune overtook them; and additional hopes that people would compassionately go beyond the basic welfare regulations. With such certainties went the overall responsibility to care for others when they were experiencing bad times. Given that the rights had to be respected by all, the system was viable without the massive bureaucratic welfare state that we are burdened with.

Tools of business:
Interest, Business Finance and Entrepreneurial Activity
Ancient principles behind loan and interest rules have been examined in Chapter 2 and, in Chapter 3 was a modern understanding of this same idea, that *real credit* resides in the collective success of a whole nation, rather than in the *financial credit* residing in the money of the lender. This explained the logic of the ban on interest on loans, because people were not to be charged by other individuals for that which everyone's combined success had made possible. It led on to the possibilities for the reform of modern banking systems that is, of capturing for the community the *real credit* currently taken by banks as they create money in the modern economy.

Interest
Here are examined some of the effects likely if interest on loans at the retail and personal level was not charged. A discouragement or outright banning of interest for business ventures, would encourage those with spare capital to consider equity (shareholding) finance for entrepreneurial activity if they wanted a gain on their money, which would help the profitability of ventures. Marginally profitable ventures would have a greater chance of succeeding and more entrepreneurial activity would be assisted, to the benefit of employment and the general economy. In our times, where there is an option to choose between safe interest-bearing deposits as a home for spare capital and riskier entrepreneurial investment, the safer choice precludes much entrepreneurial activity which cannot afford the burden of interest charges. Any move to encourage the use of equity capital for the promotion of business and, or, to discourage interest

bearing debt is to be welcomed. In the extreme case a general ban on interest would clearly do this, as deposited money would have no function in attracting wealth but merely become a convenient store of it to be drawn upon for consumption as required. Interest is banned in Islam under Sharia Law and was banned for Christians for the first half of the Christian era. With a ban on interest a lender might be more considerate about the needs of the poor, such as in helping them to establish a business.

Profit sharing

What alternatives are there to loans without interest, apart from shareholding? The skills of employees, after salary payments, could bring them profit-sharing (along with the owner of the capital). Free share options are a way of acknowledging what might be called the 'personal capital value' that has been built up. The risk of capital loss would be carried by the richer, but rewards (dividends) would accrue for all who had a financial or 'personal capital' stake in the business. Shareholding as a general idea, by excluding the burden of repayment from the borrower, and in bringing a share of the reward to all, could be seen as having features of mutuality discussed in Chapter 1. They can be a device that brings people into a stronger relationship, at least on small scale ventures where people know each other. The Scott Bader Commonwealth (Appendix C) is a successful industrial company that has been running for fifty years with its employees as members of a 'commonwealth'.

Employment Bonds

The R Foundation of Cambridge is arranging for the funding of ventures which bring employment through interest-free 'Employment Bonds' for schemes in certain cities and regions, by asking individuals and groups to forgo interest on repayable loans in the cause of the unemployed finding work. Also, the Prince's Trust through its grants to new businesses displays the kind of action expected to be normal to those following Mosaic principles. Grants have similarities to the land assets of a pastoral system, since they can be a vital foundation of future success.

But the scarcity of such schemes is in great contrast to the traditional capitalist way of loading the odds in favour of those who already have spare assets. The system expected that all would be entrepreneurial, and *those with assets were expected to carry the risks* as they helped the poor back into successful self-reliance again. Now, most of us never give a personal business enterprise a serious thought because of the expense and risks involved and because few have the readily available assets, or want to risk the few assets they have. Our economic culture has a risk emphasis opposite to the Mosaic one: for us the risks to the rich and the large are reduced and the risks to the poor and small are increased. Which confirms the Lottery Principle: *'the poor create the rich'.*

To forgo interest on a business loan, would be a seen as a generous act (or possibly, nonsense) according to the norms of modern Western society, and if associated with equity investment and advice, would be a sign of a developed entrepreneurial attitude and a trusting relationship. But such enlightened entrepreneurial arrangements can only really work if the general financial bias were to be monolithically against interest payments or if relationships in business were more truly co-operative. This again points to a Mosaic principle, the one needing the money or credit is known and knows the one providing it, which is a safeguard and a help to both. Growing and long-standing relationships were at the heart of those enlightened ways and any legislation that builds on them to help employment and entrepreneurial activity is to be encouraged.

Banking

It is a very convenient practice to leave money with a bank which can then lend it on to others who are unknown to the depositor. The money is secure and available, there is a regular reward of interest and one does not have to deal personally with other people who need money. The lack of a personal link between the one with spare capital and the user of it removes part of the dynamic of a truly human system. Financial help in those times was principally available from related or known individuals, which factor is important to both parties. The lender would, on the strength of the relationship rather than the credit rating of the borrower, view the situation with some compassion despite the possibility of the debt being written off in the future. The borrower would be obliged not to abuse the element of trust and help. With modern banking however, on the one hand bank officials are under a primary obligation to the shareholders, and matters of personal feeling towards the borrower and their need for capital are secondary. So the dynamics of modern banking begin with the protection of the capital of those who have it to the detriment of those who do not. The ability to give practical help to others who are handling a faltering business, is not usually possible within modern banking.

Moses' aims were to help the losers to become producers again and to guard against them being exploited. Both his system and ours are concerned with the preservation of assets. Ours has mechanisms aiding those who hold assets now, so that they might preserve them. Moses' had mechanisms for all, to keep their minimal assets, to increase their general wealth, or to recover their assets if they became separated from them.

B. NETWORKS and HIEIRACHCIES

Relationships: Who is my neighbour?

The basic social unit in every successful society on the planet is the family, within the extended family, within local and regional groupings. The family is the secure base for normal life and has been the channel for help to the less fortunate in every society throughout history until modern times with the rise of state welfare. In the Mosaic model without a central government as such, the law granted assets and other financial rights to all families and individuals irrespective of merit, and established people so that they could independently provide for their own, and enable them to carry out their responsibilities to others. The relationship between rights and responsibilities is a delicate one. To have responsibilities without rights is oppressive. It would be progress for our society to acknowledge personal and family financial rights for all, to ensure personal survival first, and thereafter the means to help others.

The nuclear family - a modern oddity

Moses' social policy strengthened family links as a priority. The land secured people in their family groups within which the productive life of the nation developed and the weak or disadvantaged, whether young or old, were cared for in a wide natural network. In our times such support is recognised through the giving of state benefits to families. But bolder solutions are needed to enable people to help members of their own families and friends but who cannot, due to a variety of reasons, such as time constraints, the need to earn for themselves or the lack of suitable accommodation. So many older citizens, for example, live in segregated housing away from their normal community life and away from their families, for want of quite simple solutions. As mentioned earlier an example might be more imaginative accommodation aided if necessary by the relaxation of planning rules, and tax relief or grants. Importantly the Citizens Royalty would enable some welfare provision to be funded by the family. The modern Western economy, which demands high mobility of employees, dislocates family groupings that were usually local. Although improved communications of all sorts obviously help to lessen the impact of distance, there are many situations where proximity of location is essential to the support and care that in the ancient scheme of things came from blood-related people. The trend to smaller and scattered families results in fewer related carers and helpers for the weak and old, and adds to the need for assistance from the state as carer of last resort.

Mosaic capitalism: co-operation across networks

We are far removed from the dynamic of the pastoral economy and one difference is the specialisation of skills, which has been a contributing factor to material and technological progress. The ancient society retained an egalitarian dynamic, as long as the more successful respected the laws regarding debt and employment release, and land restoration. The 'neighbour' of *'love your neighbour as yourself'* was any citizen, clearly most often those geographically close by and related through family ties, but not solely so. Everyone had similar basic economic rights in the medium and long term and this prevented the formation of permanent hierarchies that are normal in most other societies.

A family or group of friends is a small model of the network. It makes almost every decision informally as and when needed, it forms and re-forms itself and follows leadership from within itself in response to changing pressures, creating whatever temporary low level hierarchy is needed. It respects leadership and authority in other individuals according to their level of experience and track record, and for reasons of efficiency. The roles of prime mover and supporter, leader and follower can swap frequently between the same people depending on the task and depends not a little on the good relationships between the individuals concerned. Network marketing is an example of how networks can work successfully in business.

By contrast, hierarchical systems necessarily need formal procedures and fixed protocols at all times so that all know their place and function, as part of a controlled system. This is not to say that some hierarchies are not inevitable and essential even within networks, as individuals by experience or skill find themselves leading groups in hierarchical patterns. Hierarchies enable the attainment of goals that might be impossible otherwise and herein lies their advantage and their danger. Strong hierarchies are useful for achieving results for people focussed around a common cause, such as political action, profits for shareholders, or victory in war. They achieve most when led by inspired people who can imbue others with vision. They are wasteful and ineffective when the hierarchy itself becomes the largest focus and rules take precedence over purpose. The need for management consultants to reshape businesses is evidence that hierarchical patterns are often too rigid to reshape themselves as required by changing goals. Perhaps it is helpful to see both network and hierarchy in terms of the other, as they both can be appropriate devices at various times. A regularly reforming hierarchy may approximate to a successful network.

Imbalances of power, due to imbalances of income and asset ownership mean that hierarchical patterns prevail in society as the big players look after their own interests, with the rest falling into line down the hierarchy. However, start everyone with equal assets and networks of mutually interdependent people might arise, with less need for expensive state-provided welfare. But to what extent do societies desire to move towards a fairer asset spread?

Modern capitalism and hierarchies

With the industrialisation that accompanied early modern capitalism, the agriculturally-based society was necessarily going through rationalisation as improvements in technology brought massive change. The enclosure movement had been progressing for centuries and ancient rights to common fields were mostly a memory. The small strips that families used for cultivation were amalgamated and the families who up to that point had been semi-independent were forced to become employed labourers. The consolidated landholdings brought efficient farming and profits, and their high value facilitated the raising of capital for the new industrial ventures and foreign trade. All this was standard agricultural and financial practice; but as to who *owned* the improved estate whether it was one family or every family who might once have tenanted the small parts, was a legal and ultimately a political matter. The law decided that the smallholders and common-field users were tenants only. Previously the agricultural tenants at least had some independence through their smallholding. Whether as labourers on the new large farms or in the new factories, the displaced farmers found themselves in hierarchical relationships in place of their previously more independent working lifestyle. Many family sized Free Lunches based on ancient land rights were lost to many people as they were consolidated into the hands of a few. The hierarchies of the factories did not sit well with ideas of interdependence and mutuality. They encouraged subservience and dependency, and at worst they were oppressive.

Socialism and hierarchies

Those advocating socialism, at its foundation, appealed variously to the notion of 'The Brotherhood of Man' and sometimes to the Sermon on the Mount, of Jesus Christ. But they did not go far enough to the practical underlying political and economic ideas of Moses. Many of the early socialists acknowledged inspiration from Henry George with his insights into the causes of poverty, but they failed to follow through in practice, believing more in the class-based ideas of Marx. Henry George would not have welcomed the growth of the collectivist state that the socialist experiment embarked upon for the next century.

Although the welfare state has achieved some alleviation of poverty, it has had to be funded by what are in effect 'enforced charitable donations' known to us as 'taxation'. But the associated managed economy and collectivist arrangements are at variance with an ideal of government dispersed to the people. Powerful hierarchies are needed to operate centrally organized states, and the cost and dynamic of these frustrate the opportunities for individuals to become self-reliant. Not that many problems of unfettered capitalism have not been addressed by socialistic activity, but the idea that a government at the centre can plan around the creativity of the individual, the family, or the local grouping, is ultimately not tenable.

At best the socialist way gives no long-term answers, with the need for and expense of high levels of welfare even in good economic times. It also brings its own problems such as the curtailment of freedom, and it can be as oppressive as capitalistic hierarchies are. Inevitably the largesse promoted by the socialistic centre must be targeted for reasons of economy at a limited number of priority groups to the exclusion of others, and to the dissatisfaction of those who have to pay the taxes. The truly radical way ofy empowering all and encouraging small unit interdependence cuts away both socialistic and capitalistic types of hierarchy. Many of their associated problems would not arise under such reforms.

A new solution is needed which empowers individuals, a system that enhances natural networks and groupings. Capitalism is the natural vehicle for enterprise, but what is needed is a different version of capitalism. One that brings to individuals, families and other small groupings the modern equivalent of the financial security that in a pastoral society land ownership brought, so that all can become self-supporting contributors. These ideas sit awkwardly with heavily centralised and bureaucratic government, apart from some such legislation to keep the system up to date and fair.

Diffused ownership and complex technology

What is the difficulty of workers being owners, and owners being workers? The division of labour, a feature of the industrial society, is a matter of practical efficiency. But such a practice need bear no relationship to the *ownership* of commercial firms, as various cooperative, and shareholder-worker models testify (such as Scott Bader and John Lewis).

But it is rare in our time for all workers and staff in a large business to own it; usually the chance to gain extra wealth through ownership is limited to a few top executives and managers. There seems no reason why an economy vested in land, agriculture and simple crafts having a fundamentally even and fair ownership could not have developed into an industrial one with similar ownership patterns. The key is the political will to deal seriously with the inevitable rule, by default, of the Lottery Principle whereby *'the poor create the rich'*.

C. RHYTHMS: Chaotic or planned?

Family voting rights

In Chapter 2 the Mosaic society was seen to have had a long term view, given the fifty and seven year, land and debt laws. Whereas in terms of practical economic and business management in our time a view beyond two years is very sketchy, in those days the people were to be used to looking far into the future. One generation might 'lose' some land but the next would gain it back and this reminder would bring a sense of hope for the future to everyone. For the medium term the seven year cycles of debt and employment limits would reinforce this. In our day the long term view might be fostered with family voting rights (see Chapter 7).

Nature's cycles

We are all hostage to rhythms of climate, weather and seasons; years months, weeks and days; light and dark. It is a measure of what has been achieved through centuries of material progress that we can override some of them. Ingenuity has extended the possibilities of activity that would otherwise be curbed by failing daylight or prevented by climatic extremes. This has raised economic growth and helped bring some technological benefits to more people, sooner, and more plentifully, than would have been otherwise.

Disparities and business cycles

Vilfredo Pareto (1849-1923), an Italian sociologist and economist postulated that in any society over time a disproportional amount of its total income gravitates to a minority of its people. This is a confirmation of the Lottery Principle. David Hume (1711-1776), the philosopher and economist, observed the same trend with respect to property ownership in general. The Mosaic system of cyclically based correcting measures based around unalienable economic rights were devices that would counter and moderate these effects.

The work of the Russian economist, Nikolai Kondratiev (d. 1938) in the 1920s revealed the natural rhythms of long business cycles repeating at intervals of around forty-five to sixty years, over recent centuries. They are characterized by periods which alternate between rising and then falling levels of prices, and variations in economic growth. Runs of prosperous years are followed by recessions or slumps that throw many into unemployment. There is much awareness of these modern business cycles so perhaps Mosaic ideas could relate to them. That system not only gave careful attention to the harnessing of individual creativity but seem also to have acknowledged powerful rhythms running down the years through society and made space for them. What happens today is that our governments and central bankers attempt to *tame or eliminate* these rhythms, imagining that steady and uninterrupted growth is possible. But an early investigator of business cycles, the French economist Clement Juglar (1889), pointed out that the boom following a sharp downturn is likely to have added vigour, whereas a weak recession is followed by feeble growth.

Recession or recreation?

We dread slumps and recessions, but Moses *planned for some work breaks and stipulated their timing,* using them for rest and other activities. 'Reduced-employment' for everyone at certain times, was considered a high point in the national cultural cycle and quite opposite to our dreaded 'unemployment'. Would it not be better to *plan* for a break or a slowdown that is likely to come at some time? We not only anxiously scan the economic horizon for unpredictable downturns but also try and fight them when we think they are serious. Why not make room for them and plan accordingly so that they can do their necessary work, just as we accept natural rhythms like seasons? But perhaps our business crashes are exaggerated specifically through our neglect of the acknowledgement of basic human economic rights for all?

Secrets of the property developers
In his book *The Power in the Land*, (the principal UK work on Land Value Taxation), Fred Harrison traces property cycles repeating at approximately 18 year intervals from 1918. He points out the (usually) clear peaks of the cycles as 1918, 1935, 1955 and 1973. He was writing in 1983, and we have now seen the 1990 peak to prove the point again. With such knowledge as this, those investing in property can be guided in their dealings by an approximate foreknowledge of market movements that could be the foundation of fortunes. Writing of 1978, an intermediate peak, Harrison records the scarcity of building plots, which forced home owners to pay large proportions of their income to start them in property ownership, a typical occurrence at such times. He illustrates the way that property price 'bubbles' takes money out of the economy to the extent that consumer buying power is cut back, possibly inducing recession as witness the set-backs of the mid-1970s and early-1990s following the preceding property booms.

King Canute. Tide cycles and business cycles
Studies by Kuznets (b.1901) of the US economy indicated its cyclical pattern, particularly related to building, and covering 15 to 25 year periods; Kitchin clarified much shorter ones of 3–4 years; and Schumpeter (1883-1950) related them all to each other. The expansion of business activity which they describe gathers pace, builds up and then dies. When the property market price bubble bursts, as it does particularly spectacularly after its final surge, it has an effect on subsequent general business activity, The start and finish dates of the cycles are impossible to be precise about whilst they are occurring, Hindsight is needed to confirm the change in momentum, but there seems undeniably to be such a succession of events. The full cycle includes an up-phase of boom and a down-phase when the economy shrinks or slumps. Some politicians appear to think that they can

prevent the down phase altogether by declaring that they are skilled enough to have abolished the days of boom and bust, imagining that a smooth, even growth can go on for ever without unpleasant falls. Perhaps the lesson that King Canute received (or forced his flattering courtiers to observe) when he tried to turn the tide on a beach is one to be understood by those who absurdly imagine, or seem to say, that they can manage business cycles out of existence.

James Grant in *The Trouble with Prosperity* (Appendix C) takes the view that rather than trying to avoid downturns, these are just what are needed to force the economy to shed badly founded businesses and provide a firm platform for the next leap upward. Human beings will do foolish things in economic matters as much as in any other, and reality needs to dawn to expose faults so that the rest of us do not have to pay even more for their failure. Governments try to ameliorate their problems and Grant quotes Keynes who in 1924 in a lecture in Oxford warned that governments should take care not to introduce inflation with their unrestrained spending. Rather that they should not involve themselves with things that individuals could do themselves, but with things not being done at all.

Samuel Brittan (Appendix C) details the efforts of governments that he had observed during the period of the 1970's and early 1980's when there was a combination of roaring inflation, rocketing unemployment and low or negative growth. He mentions one government that ineptly doubled the VAT which raised inflation and wage claims just as recession was setting in. Brittan attributes the already-high inflation partly to the Oil Shock when the oil producing cartel (OPEC) raised prices in 1973. But Harrison (Appendix C) suggests that there were other factors at work at home, the regular cycle in land values should have warned of economic storms ahead, quite apart from the OPEC moves. The high demand for land and the shortages of it, and the slow planning process, were factors that Harrison suggests were key to the soaring property prices which helped, with the oil price rise, to promote the subsequent inflation.

Electoral cycles
UK governments have an advantage over US governments in that they may have the option of timing the next election rather than having dates forever set into the future. In the US the very fixity of the term may lend itself to medium term economic cycle distortion as the government might be tempted to 'manage' the natural cycling of the economic situation. Admittedly, controls in the hands of central

bankers may take away some room for political manoeuvre. Whether it is possible to achieve anything beneficial from such intervention is doubtful, as meddling often exacerbates problems. But UK governments do have a possibility of 'riding the cycle' as they allow it to work more naturally, with some possibility of timing elections around it, rather than attempting to manipulate it around fixed electoral dates. The primitive pastoral economy was to follow fixed dates as long as all agreed its pattern and without central government. Interference was not possible. The cycles were benign devices that were to bring the benefit of long term national stability and prosperity to all. Because we have no such inbuilt safeguards and disciplines, powerful people have been allowed to take advantage of the weak and poor, with the result that a major function of central government is to cope with the resulting deprivation. Unfortunately, the maintenance of such power can deaden the self-reliance and creativity of individuals, drain wealth and ensure the need for the continuation of the extensive government.

Business cycles, rest, recreation, release and restoration
It is ironic that the much vaunted freedom that commercial concerns can exercise, for instance by opening a shop seven days in a week, does not produce more profit in total for all retailing. There are, after all, no extra pay cheques being received by the buying public because retailers are open an extra day a week. The same spending merely spreads over one more day, which for the retailer means an extra day of overheads. The motive for this exercise is that aggressive retailers can take market share from other retailers by opening more opening hours in a given locality. The 'free market' has become the guiding star and we sacrifice the well-being of low earners, who need the money, so that a major retailer's shareholders can gain a small advantage, and so that we are not inconvenienced by the need to organize shopping over a few less hours per week.

Our ability to over-ride some natural cycles is taken as an imperative to do so and thereby promote uninterrupted commercial activity. The Mosaic cycles were superimposed on the natural ones. From the shortest cycle of the seventh day rest, to the more irregular religious festivals through the year, to the repeating seventh year of rest from farming work and the fiftieth year to mark the return to family land. Societies use rhythms to function well and maintain a sense of community and wellbeing. Rest-breaks and national holidays help prevent over-exploitation, as the poor are relieved of work for a while. Increasingly for us this is on an individual basis only, as the communal nature of society-wide breaks disappears with 24 hour / 7 day, activity. The right of a rest from work without undue financial penalty can be seen as a non-financial 'priceless' benefit, similar to good health. The complexity of our modern society means that a complete stop, by everyone at one time, is not possible. Hospitals and power generation must continue for life's sake, and besides, as noted, the purpose of the rest day was to bring human benefit and was not to be an end in itself. However, with such legislation as the general abolition of Sunday trading laws, the possibility of a beneficial rest for as many people as possible at the same time is fading. Many would not work unsocial hours unless it was a condition of their employment and there was little other convenient employment available. But the demand is for freedom to shop at any time, and retailers comply to enlarge their market share, thus contributing to the 'unsocial working' of some of the poorest of society. 'Unsocial' is anti-family and anti-community. One cannot as fully enjoy the positive benefits of family life or the choice of a full social life, if one is tied to working whilst most other people are not working and pursuing non-work activities. Those who are poorest have to take the least desirable jobs. There are fewer and fewer fixed days when all relax together. We are alarmed at workers in developing countries being exploited so that we can buy our fashion clothing at keen prices, and even join boycott campaigns in attempts to improve conditions. But what of the exploitation resulting because we have cut legislation to prevent universal opening hours at our local superstores?

Time choices - only for the better off
What is the objection, it might be asked, to 24/7 working if everyone working shifts takes as much time off as anyone else, as indeed, employment legislation insists upon? There are two main sufferers: small organizations and individuals working for large ones. Continuous working around industrial production lines and processes has been part of life for two centuries of capitalistic industrialization. Efficient production lines bring cheaper products which benefit all, and many such practices could not be stopped without adversely affecting some of the people most in need. But the proliferation of large supermarkets, shows the impact of such changes and demonstrates how the free market naturally almost always works against the small business. The demise of many shops in towns and of village shops is accelerated through large chains of supermarkets

opening for extended hours. This is beyond price advantage only but through their ability to finance losses so caused for as long as it takes to permanently gain the extra trade by driving smaller competitors out of business. Shift working is a feature of some services and processes which need to be kept going to make them viable and to increase their profits when they are. Worker co-operation in working non-social hours may be rewarded with extra pay, giving a monetary compensation for the loss of choice of social activity. But small firms cannot easily compete against such competition.

The 'freedom' to ignore communal holidays and submit to the pressure from shareholders to trade all hours and everyday, favours only certain people related to these large organizations. The most favoured are the shareholders; top management retain some freedom to choose their breaks, but lower down in the organization there is increasing restriction, as middle and lower management and workers find that their freedom to choose their own time for social activity is governed by the demands of the organization. Unsocial shifts may become compulsory. Here is a good reason for heeding Moses' legislation of the restriction of working time so that all can have the same periods of freedom from work, rather than be obliged to take time off to suit the organization. These social costs can be avoided by the better off, and the resulting unfairness to the poor was the reason for the Mosaic regulations. Some restriction and discipline is necessary in every society that values the human rights of all its citizens.

Game playing – the interval, communal recreation
Again it is from games that we can receive a demonstration of fairness in the case of rests and breaks. What sort of a game of football or rugby would it be if, instead of a half-time break for all, the players took their rest for a few minutes separately throughout the game? The most effective way to recover during a game is for all to stop together.

Taking time off as holiday when everyone else is doing the same brings an extra feeling of relaxation since the widespread stopping of many regular activities emphasises the change in tempo. In particular, social activities can be arranged which would be less inclusive if working life continues unchanged and unrelieved, with every day a working day, and every day a rest day for only a few in turn. Friends and families can get together and sporting events are possible. For everyone who stops work together at these times there is a psychological benefit since fewer people, customers or colleagues are at their business and creating a backlog, 'for me to clear when I get back'. Clearly in the modern economy 'recreation' is often linked to a business providing facilities for it. There is a difficulty in drawing the line between when the provision of recreation for some people, becomes exploitation for others who need the employment necessary in its provision. The earlier discussion about *having* to work at unsocial times due to poverty, rather than having more choice not to because of sufficient income, points to a solution through the provision of a basic citizen's income.

E. CAMEL SWALLOWING

Elitism in housing
Faced with runaway house prices the New Labour government in 2001 announced schemes for the assisted funding of homes by nurses, teachers and the police, to enable them to live near their places of work, using the device of shared-equity schemes. A failure to apply Henry George's solution of a tax on land values, has resulted in this introduction of elitism from a political party that was founded to promote fairness! This is admirable for the workers themselves, making life easier for them, as well as possibly setting them up with a Free Lunch through rising land prices, and it does help to keep certain public services from crisis. But it deals only with symptoms, and it is complex and bureaucratic. It ignores the root problem and makes the favoured group dependent on the state, which is unhealthy in a democracy. The scheme is described to be necessary for 'key workers', which ignores the fact that everyone is 'key' to a successful society, and that many of them have housing problems too.

Bearing in mind the above 'solution' to the particular need of affordable housing for one group of people, it is instructive to return to the earlier measure of the 'right to buy' given to council tenants (Chapter 4). This was introduced to give some people a place in the housing market but a side effect was that many houses have been withdrawn from the supply of affordable homes, leaving the poorest in a possibly more dire state of housing need than otherwise. The current (2002) government is therefore proposing that the right to buy will be curtailed in certain high housing cost areas, to 'protect' the disadvantaged from an ever-decreasing supply. This illustrates that each inadequate 'camel swallowing' measure has to be countered some time later by yet another similarly inadequate measure, all because the root problem has never clearly recognised and tackled with vigour.

Camel swallowing – modern style

Each government tries in turn to redress society's faults and failings. But inevitably most of these attempts, whilst achieving some reform, leave glaring problems unattended, and contain seeds of new problems.

It has been noted in Chapter 2 how Jesus described this tendency in his joke about 'camel swallowing'. In the same way many of the attempts by governments to 'address the problems', as in the housing example, involve repeated 'camel swallowing'.

The essence of camel swallowing is that a particular policy, is looked upon as the answer to the problem being addressed, whilst more basic and ultimately more important things are not addressed. Inevitably the solution of the day, or even the solutions to many symptoms *cannot* be the whole answer. The electorate so easily sees through the posturing that accompanies these shallow answers, that cynicism arises and politicians are held in low esteem. The challenge is to find more certain answers for society beyond the current isolated policies taken on a 'pick and mix' basis, which have little effect on the underlying problems.

Passing the buck: Employers, Employees and the Welfare State

With the growth of hierarchical capitalism and the bureaucratic state, as family and local support links have weakened, other non-family links have of necessity formed. In our culture the enduring nature of employment means that the employer's organization becomes a long term and major factor in people's lives. It takes the creative efforts of the employees for it's own ends, and gives back little more than self-interested support to the employee and often only as compelled by legislation. Gradually over the industrialised centuries, due to the need for a skilled workforce to produce a profitable company, some power has had to be shared with employees. Such things as contracts of employment, sick and holiday pay, redundancy and unemployment pay, pensions and so on, have become necessities for employers. But those who have only fleeting employment with many different employers do not so easily establish the rights that their longer term colleagues do. In both cases, managers often have limited scope for personal judgement outside narrow guidelines due to obligations to shareholders. Failing adequate provision for employees, the state has had to step in, but with rules even more restricted. The need for accountability, of necessity brings bureaucracy with its own multiplication of checks, paperwork, delay and frustration. The sense of duty and obligation of individuals to each other, which are natural within an interdependent long term community, cannot have a place within a bureaucratic welfare system. A state benefit system, due to its impersonal nature, makes fraud more possible, whereas in a 'relational' system, donors or helpers would be familiar with the circumstances of the person needing the help. This would guard against dishonesty and bring awareness of the true extent of the need.

Historically, state benefits developed out of locally based schemes (in the UK the Poor Law). Local charitable schemes such as the building of almshouses for the poor achieved some relief. But these were based on granting charity rather than recognizing rights. Conditions would be what those who ran the schemes paternalistically decided upon. Ultimately the system became heartless and inadequate and the burden of relief was taken up nationally by the state, bringing distant, bureaucratic and expensive solutions to local and individual problems. At best some evenness of poor relief resulted, but at the same time a principle was introduced in removing concern for the disadvantaged from the network of their local acquaintances. When there is a state-run safety-net available, a person needing help can merely be seen as a problem to be dealt with by an official, rather than a fellow human being who needs help. The high cost of welfare entails targeting benefits and the means-testing of applicants to ensure that money only goes where intended. Tax credits aimed at encouraging people get back to work makes the bureaucratic burden fall increasingly on the employer. Such processes are complex and may adversely affect the take up of the targeted benefit. On the other hand a working family tax credit introduced in 1999 is having bizarre effects. At certain low levels of income it does encourage people into part-time work due to the part-time 'pay and benefit' package, but it can inhibit them from going full-time due to a drop in income for more hours work. It is even causing full-time low earners to cut their hours! Whilst this could be a benefit to some families who would prefer to be with their children for longer, it remains to be seen if this is actually the intention of the legislation, or whether the rules will be qualified by extra bureaucratic conditions.

Scoring goals – own goals

Many 'answers' to some of these problems can be self-defeating. The legislation to protect worker's rights in the event of takeover known as the Transfer of Undertakings for the Protection of Employment (TUPE) was commented on in an article by John Jay in *The Sunday*

Times (7 May 2000). The raising of the limit of any claim for unfair dismissal from £12,000 to £50,000 looks like a good deal for employees. If a change in conditions of employment after a business sale could be deemed to be 'constructive dismissal', the new employer could find themselves paying out large amounts in compensation. But the possibility of such high costs could so reduce the sale value that it might be more profitable to break up the business completely with possible complete loss of employment, rather than sell it on as a going concern.

The Soup Kitchen

For people who never eat at the Free Lunch Restaurant, The Soup Kitchen
may be essential to their survival.

But don't think that you can just arrive and be served.
Many conditions will have to be met before you arrive at the counter for your soup.
There is an obstacle course to negotiate
involving hoops to climb through, hurdles to jump, walls to climb
and unpleasant and demeaning tasks to endure.
But with persistence you may be able to succeed in getting free soup regularly.

Increasingly, some of the people who benefit from The Soup Kitchen
would have seemed out of place when it was founded
For example, business executives who persuade the management that they are a
worthy cause, are given soup in bulk.
Some people are sent with their soup to the Free Lunch Restaurant
and provided with a shared table there.

Nevertheless some people, after having filled in all the entry forms
for which The Soup Kitchen is famous, find that they seem to be in a special category
which the management has either not foreseen, or decided to ignore.

Even in good times, the cost of running The Soup Kitchen keeps rising.
Worryingly, some of the Free Lunchers who have to contribute towards its overheads
are needing to go to there themselves.

Because both The Restaurant and The Soup Kitchen have been around for so long
few people ever wonder whether there might be a better way of feeding people,
than the choice between such extremes in the same town.

Similarly, the more recent legislation on employers to provide pensions if their employees demand them might also have the effect of shutting some firms down altogether, or preventing new ones from getting started. The same government that is promoting these new pension plans, in 1997 cut a time-honoured tax advantage for income received from pension fund investments by 20% at a stroke! The cash refund of tax that had been pre-paid on dividends, was stopped, and pensioners lose £5bn assistance per year thereby.

How long can this bizarre dance go on?
The way in which the state reacts with the citizen as both taxpayer and promoter of wealth, might be portrayed as a strange dance between two characters wherein each is attracted to, yet repelled by, the other. Whether with corporate business, or with individual citizen, attempts are made to make everyone increasingly socially accountable due to the failings of the system. The state makes demands on business and citizen's resources - time and tax being the most obvious. As firms comply with, and resist these measures, they become loaded with expensive costs that can kill the golden goose of business enterprise that is the prime source of the wealth. The resulting unemployment leads to both citizens and businesses becoming dependent on state handouts and European Union grants. However due to their complexity and poor accessibility due to bureaucratic barriers, the process often requires specialist knowledge to access.

Consultants set themselves up as latter day Robin Hoods to take resources from the rich state and deliver them to firms and individuals. Whereas accountants advise clients on *minimizing* tax (i.e. repelling the state's demands), these consultants advise on *maximizing* grants (i.e. attracting the state's gifts). With the state taking away and restricting with one hand, and giving back with the other, a threat is posed to democracy as well as to wealth creation. The losses due to fraud and the waste of administration in government, accountancy and grant consultancy mean that every taxpayer is paying for services that contribute nothing to the wealth of society. These schemes are rarely aimed to help foster the small business - regardless of the fact that much future wealth will come from them. Whilst larger firms might eventually tap a £100,000 or £1m grant, a self-employed individual is unlikely ever to be given even £2,000.

The cultural conditioning of the welfare state is to assume that someone else will take care of the unemployed and the low earners, and because of this we are limited psychologically as well as financially by the cost of the system to each of us. Compassion once institutionalised in this way, weakens fellow feeling between people. The lower and the higher paid become alienated from each other when the practical expression of compassion is made difficult, in this case by the very system that was set up to provide care! Our system has become unbalanced, since there are so many who are relatively poor and need help. 'The poor will always be with you' is taken as read, but *why so many* poor? Those receiving state help usually need more than the cash handout of the welfare state; they need the personal support that people can give in order to lead them into greater self-support. This help relies on good relationships as being fundamental to the well-being of society but, as noted, the socialistic welfare solutions need rigid hierarchies and strict control which are unhelpful in such matters. The welfare system has become so widespread and the administrative burden so expensive that a Citizen's Royalty looks increasingly attractive for reasons of simplicity and greater effectiveness.

Who needs a tax shelter if it isn't raining taxes?

It has long been socialist dogma to treat high earnings as 'monopoly' situations where people are earning 'economic rent' which should be targeted with high taxation. But taxes for high earners have gradually become taxes for all earners as the most powerful monopoly of all, land, has worked its poverty-sustaining effects, which always ensures that much welfare is needed. Ever higher demands are made on even modest incomes and on everyday goods and services, as the costs of the state keep rising, especially under governments that are predisposed to providing services divorced from the practicalities and realities of markets. This self-perpetuating circle of deprivation will continue to race round quite unhindered for as long as the most effective taxation against poverty, that on land value, is ignored.

Today 40% of the national product is taken in tax from companies and individuals. Not only is this a financial burden, but increasingly businesses have to work as unpaid tax collectors/benefit dispensers, thus wasting productive time and increasing their overheads. The outpouring of taxation legislation increases the cost of expensive advice to minimise tax liability, which rises with every layer and twist of legislation. Hidden accounts with nominee labels disappear to the distant shores of tax shelters and havens like the Isle of Man and the Cayman Islands which means that some of a wealthy citizen's capital is less available for spending in the mother country. A radical simplification of the system is needed that would benefit the whole economy. Tax avoidance, whether of the 'cash-only' or tax haven varieties would become increasingly irrelevant with Land Value Tax as a single tax in place of income tax and VAT, etc, since LVT cannot be avoided. Under this simpler system, action against fraud would be more effective. Accountants who now largely deal with taxation would be able to concentrate on activities more financially beneficial to businesses such as management accounting.

Privatisation

Leyland Bus was sold in early 1987 to its management and financiers for £4m, debt free. It was sold on, less than eighteen months later, for £20m. Cosmo Graham and Tony Prosser (Appendix C. *Privatising Public Enterprises*) tell of this and other deals which failed to maximise returns for the public purse.

Privatisation, the dismantling of the nationalisation set up in the long political experiment of the 20th century, enforces competition and brings some price and service benefits to consumers. But the organizations concerned were financed through many decades by taxpayers, both at their original nationalisation and for their ongoing investment. As the only resources governments have are from its taxpaying citizens, so privatisation sold the organizations back to the owners, or at least those owners who were able to afford to buy them! Some did so, and at low prices, thus helping to promote what Pareto observed, that over time, high incomes accumulate in fewer hands.

As mentioned in chapter 3 there are other ways of handling privatisation which would benefit everyone rather than the favoured few.

Mutuality

The building societies of today had their origin over 200 years ago. Groups of people entered into a self-help arrangement whereby all saved into a common fund to buy materials with which they could build a house for one of their number. The person who was chosen by vote to take the first house would still contribute the agreed amount into the fund until everyone had their dwelling in turn. At this point the 'terminating' building society was disbanded. From this idea came the 'permanent' building society (the most famous being The Halifax, founded in 1852), which received the savings of those who already owned their own houses. Similarly the Co-operative idea enables small operators to survive through mutual support. The idea of customers being owners, and sellers and buyers sharing profits, has an inherent fairness about it. The UK has seen the recent demise of many mutually run Building Societies with their conversion into banks, albeit now owned by earlier 'members' as shareholders. But the benefits of favourable interest rates for lenders and borrowers are reduced because of the added demands of the new shareholders needing a dividend. The origins of Building Societies were based on the need for reasonably priced finance for borrowers, and fair, safe investment income for lenders. However Land Value Tax could have a much greater impact on wider home homeownership than Building Society 'mutuality' ever will.

Microcredit

The financing of small businesses in the developing world through small loans by the device known as Microcredit is of the same tradition of Credit Unions which have an honoured history for over 100 years. Monitoring of the borrower's performance by a peer group is proving successful and has encouraging elements of local interdependence. Microcredit can bring financial stamina that individuals would find hard to achieve alone. But it does rely on the largesse of an outside agency to provide the capital, and involves interest payments and the repayment of capital, all of which follow traditional capitalistic lines. It clearly helps, but addresses just one of the problems that the poor are subject to.

Insurance

When a random misfortune occurs to someone in a simple and supportive community which has no insurance, those unaffected might help the unfortunate. The problem would be handled in proportion to the need, within the capabilities of those helping, so that the shortfall would be made up and no-one would suffer too much, or, conversely, many would suffer a little, which is a kind of insurance 'in arrears'. Conventional insurance can be seen as a 'reverse Lottery Principle' or 'Free Lunch in adversity' whereby many contribute ('lose') a little to cover the large losses of a few. In many countries insurance has developed to cover such losses, and removes much of the need for charitable help from the community. Cash set aside in premiums before the event, can be seen to be a way in which people who are 'related' solely through their premiums, protect themselves. But insurance is outside the influence of interpersonal relationships so that the recompense for an insured loss has to be strictly according to contract terms. Here again, as with banking customers, before the interest of policy holders is the shareholders' interest, who will require that as little is paid out as legally possible, subject to the retention of goodwill among policyholders. Compassion and duty, characteristics of a strong community, generally have no place in these commercial arrangements. Insurance does encourage responsibility, so that each looks after whatever they have, rather than having constantly to look to others or the state after suffering misfortune. It is a useful device for a sophisticated and economically successful society and those within it who can afford the premiums; but certain risks are uninsurable and will always be the province of government even in wealthy nations.

On the level of basic health care, the fact that the poorest would not be able to provide insurance premiums for privately run health care is an argument for a 'free at the point of use' National Health Service (NHS). The incidence of poverty is unlikely to shift much due to the presence of mutually self-defeating pressures within our economic system unless reforms like those suggested within these pages are introduced. Thus the lower paid, and many of the rest are certain to need such provision. But the funding and organizational culture of the NHS are the result of the socialist mindset of its founders, and its performance and outcome are poor. This is becoming evident as comparison with other models in other countries shows.

If a Citizen's Royalty recycled wealth directly to everyone, instead of to the state on everyone's behalf, alternative funding possibilities could open up for some of the services the state currently provides. People would find that they had greater choice and the services would become more sensitive to the need. Socialism has had its turn and has been seen to be badly wanting. Who can possibly manage so massive an organization as the NHS?

Free markets: can these really be possible?
Some would advocate that all that is needed is to lift restrictions on markets and allow their benefits to flow to all. In certain ways the system of Chapter 2 runs with this idea, but only after certain fundamental safeguards. The next chapter spells out some practical measures that would ensure that many more of us could start to partake fairly in 'free' markets. The flaw in the philosophy of completely unfettered market is that many of those whom the markets fail become permanently disadvantaged and that the market has no mechanism to address this problem.

The combination of 'market and state' known as the mixed economy, has not only failed the poor, but loads the rest of us with huge costs. To expect that this problem might be 'solved' by more of the same - conventional taxes and charity - when many decades of experiment have shown otherwise, is surely obvious to anyone who can look dispassionately at the results. The continuous and fussy tinkering with isolated issues, only enlarges the swallowed camel at every gulp of new regulation. A radical look at the camel itself is needed.

7

CITIZENISATION
(Loosening the grip of the Lottery Principle)

HOW INCOMPATIBLE IS FREEDOM WITH FAIRNESS?   As noted, the freedom to open shops at all hours of day and night whilst bringing choice to shoppers and extra market share to large retailers, can restrict the family and social lives of the low income shop assistants who desperately need work.   On the other hand the old Soviet-type states denied some basic individual freedoms in the cause of a spurious equality. There may be some extreme champions of freedom who will object to basic rights for all because someone's freedom will be involuntarily diminished by the change.

Democracies attempt to maximize both freedom and fairness and the inevitable tension is only resolved with the political swings back and forth over time. Unfortunately, as noted, inequality both of wealth and of opportunity (the two are somewhat related) remain stubbornly constant over many years. The poor results of different experimentation by expensive governments will, for the libertarian, prove that governments should withdraw and leave people to work out their own lives using their own resources with which governments are so profligate at present.   The arguments of these pages have a lot in common with this view *as long as some basic rights can be guaranteed for all.* With this safeguard, people should be given the chance to make some of their own mistakes rather than just to observe those of governments as they use such huge amounts of their money in their service.

But how can we be sure that by returning some power to the citizen, and reducing state power will be an improvement?   In this chapter various threads of an argument are drawn together: that behind the commonplace exhortation: *'love your neighbour as yourself'*, there are principles about fairness and freedom with practical measures to promote these qualities.   These ideas will be placed in the context of empowering citizens.

The single panacea mindset

The danger of any system that promotes a 'master plan' for society is that it is regarded as a panacea for all ills. Bitter wrangles over this or that individual case of failure of the Health Service imply that the system should not fail, *it should be the panacea.* Prime Minister Tony Blair, of New Labour, spoke of a 'big tent' idea of government to which everyone might subscribe. The idea seems to be that everyone will find a place and fulfillment in the one (presumably enduring) New Labour fold. This book proposes a different view. Instead of a 'big tent' providing for all the people, we need as many 'tents' as there are people. Instead of the one panacea for all ills, we need as many remedies as there are people. Instead of the state deciding all the answers, citizen need to decide their own solutions, and to be given the resources to empower them to do so. Questions need to be put from a different point of view. Rather than imagining that sorting management failure in public services is the main purpose of government, and that the choice for the citizen is of choosing the party that can manage the state machine most efficiently, people need to be asked: How would you like to be empowered? As an individual? As a family? In a group?

It is not only state services that are a cause of concern. Large and respected firms in business and commerce can collapse or be taken over with the loss of thousands of jobs, shareholder wealth and pension income. Is there no other way to safeguard people from the uncertainties that ensue when such wealth is shown to be so ephemeral? Whether it is the size of the organizations or the nature of the products being handled that are the problem, clearly something is beyond many of those who try and manage them, who are paid massively for their services. But when these same high-flying executives are able to leave even their failures with hundreds of thousands of pounds in a 'golden goodbye' and with generous pensions to boot, something seems seriously amiss. Before their collapse banks have poured in money to support these capitalistic champions. That banks rarely fail themselves is perhaps due to the scale of the profits they make from the creation of the credit that they supply, as has been seen in Chapter 3. The additional security of knowing that they themselves will probably be bailed out by government if they look like collapsing could also be engendering a careless attitude in their backing of some ventures.

The problem of the ultimate 'preserver of poverty', the land values which climb inexorably during every economic boom preventing the poor from owning real estate property, keeping their rents high and sucking wealth away from the productive economy, has never been tackled with sufficient logic and purpose (Chapters 4 & 5).

It is time to look for alternatives to the old left and right 'solutions' in order that the imbalances and unfairness in our society might be modified to bring greater freedom and choice to all. The underlying economic principles examined (Chapter 2) showed a system that carefully considered the economic rights of everyone. This book asserts that there is a *moral* case to be made and that there are *practical* measures to be implemented (Chapters 3 & 4) so that such ideas could become normative for social policy in our time.

Chapter 6 has shown how ineffectual are the outcomes of the policies aimed at reducing poverty. A better response to complex means testing for welfare distribution, is not to add more complexity. The answers of this book point to simpler and more effective ideas.

Resources as a right

The process by which the citizen, and the citizen's point of view, starts to take a more central role can appropriately be named *citizenisation*. Citizenisation involves the empowerment of the individual, vitally with cash.

This is not to say that the financial payments of the Citizen's Royalty should be *granted*: they should be *acknowledged as rights*. *Grants* are given as a 'gift' following the meeting of certain conditions. The grantor is in a position of power over the recipient, for instance when the Prince's Trust, the government, or the European Union give grants. *Rights* are acknowledged to be already existing and the arguments in Chapter 3 and 4 about the rights of everyone to the wealth they have been instrumental in creating, are central to the moral case for citizenisation. The payment of a regular Citizen's Royalty to each person, would emphasize to all, the equality of their citizenship.

The need for this purposeful empowerment of the citizen is an admission that the socialist experiment of the last hundred years has been shown to be inadequate both in banishing poverty and the means to greater freedom.

Over a century ago Henry George championed the cause of the citizen, but his solutions did not depend on the establishment of the socialist state. It is time to take his message to heart for the genius it contains. *Nationalisation* was the socialistic mechanism used for much of the 20th century, to be followed by *privatisation* that attempted to engage the citizen again in the wealth process. *Citizenisation* extends this idea to acknowledge rights, particularly financial rights, for all.

Citizenisation is not an encouragement to selfish individualism. Such a characteristic is more likely to be fostered by the way our system demands a large personal time commitment in the pursuit of survival, and takes so much of our income that we are less able personally to help the disadvantaged. 'What is in it for me?', is an entirely valid question inherent in 'love your neighbour as yourself'. The point is to extend the question, so that it naturally grows to: 'What is also in it for my children, and my grandchildren; my parents and my grandparents; and my friends and neighbours?' Here is an opportunity to strengthen relationship within and outside the family, empowering citizens and with money to help to make that happen.

The cash of the Royalty would, hopefully, by acknowledging citizen's *rights* first, lead on to remind of citizen's *responsibilities* and foster new responsible roles. This is in contrast to the rights of 'customers', 'clients', and 'consumers' which define many relationships in modern life.

1. CITIZEN'S ROYALTY

Unless the payment of the Citizen's Royalty is associated with 'citizenisation' as a concept, the word deserves to be ignored as an empty and largely meaningless soundbite.

The ideal first source to fund the Citizen's Royalty would be the reform of banking, whereby government through the central bank takes the profit on the issue of money rather than the banking sector. The diversion of the entire amount of this profit to the people directly, could give a Royalty of around £800 per head per annum. (Chapter 3). The alternative, to direct the proceeds of banking reform just to reduce conventional taxes, would merely benefit the better off and leave the non-taxpaying poor in their poverty. Politically, banking reform would seem a popular and least disruptive place to start since the numbers of people benefiting would far outweigh those currently profiting, who, anyway, would be generally able to fend for themselves. Banking reform represents a new largely untapped source of revenue. Being the initial source of the Royalty, it would also play an educational role and prepare the way for people to understand and accept the principle behind it: that of recycling wealth from society-generated and natural resources, to all. As Land Value Tax will have a greater and variable impact, the benefit of a previously established Citizen's Royalty funded by banking reform would smooth its way.

Sharing the cake

There is a hugely valuable national 'cake' which everyone has a part in making. It is always on the menu at the Free Lunch Restaurant. It is to wealth, what roast beef is to England, curry is to India and pasta is to Italy.

The cake represents the total sum of all land values that grow larger almost every year. This is because as our society and economy flourishes some people use their extra money to buy a house for the first time, or trade up into a bigger one. This flow of new money causes all land values to rise automatically thus enlarging the 'land value cake'.

Although our society's success is due to everyone's efforts, the wealth of this cake is only divided between the freeholders. Renters who can never jump on the property ladder and buy their own home will never get a share in the cake, although they are contributing no less to the success that lifts the prices.

If the value of all land was taxed (excluding the value of any buildings on the land), some of this community inspired wealth could be shared out fairly to everyone via a regular Citizen's Royalty and mean that other taxes could be drastically reduced or abolished.

The reform would have other beneficial effects such as bringing empty homes onto the market, reducing housing shortages, making homes more affordable and saving green fields.

Land Value Tax does not deprive anyone of anything that they have produced by their own skill, as income tax and most conventional taxes do, as they confiscate profit gained from success. How odd this is! LVT is not inspired by envy, rather it is inspired by basic justice. It is a fundamental right to receive a share in any success you have had a part in creating.

It might be objected that to use land wealth though recycling it, is to spend capital as income. But land itself is not capital, in economic terms. Capital represents humanly produced wealth formed by the application of labour and materials. Land, by contrast, like all natural resources, is a part of the planet and was, in the agrarian economy, used for everyday survival, that is, like income. The *monetary value* of land in our time can be so used for everyday survival, just as land practically is, or was, in a pastoral society.

The essential *justice* behind the levying of Land Value Tax, or the capturing of the profit from money creation, cannot be over-emphasised. No one likes the idea of 'welfare scroungers' who take benefits that others have provided, and contribute little themselves;

but this is just what happens for anyone who owns land! Whether they are the ordinary homeowners of just one house, a property developer, or a landed family with a huge property portfolio, the appreciating wealth represented by their land's value originates solely from the success of society as a whole. They may have improved the house and thereby raised *its* value, but they themselves can do nothing to change the value of the land itself. It is only demand for land from the economically successful wider society that does that for them. And here is the moral issue; even those who have no freehold themselves are contributing to all gains of the freeholders, simply by being a part of the success. Until this is appreciated by enough of us to make a political difference, a fundamental injustice will remain, and the division of our society that exists and the heavy burden of the relief of the poverty of those who are excluded, will grow.

The sharing of the land values would not be through the redistribution of physical land between all citizens, which would be inappropriate; nor through the nationalisation of land by the state, which would be unnecessary; but simply in the sharing out evenly between citizens of some of the wealth in all land plots, using the Land Value Tax to collect and the Citizens Royalty to distribute. The aim is to encourage the citizen to provide for themselves and given them their share of the wealth that they have had a part in making. The payment of the Citizen's Royalty might provide a foothold for many in the wealth-creating process. Several combined Royalties, of a family for example, could be used to fund capital borrowing for a small business venture to empower them in the way that land does in a pastoral economy. But at least the Royalty would bring a little more basic security to everyone.

But why should everyone have such a Royalty when some clearly would have no need of it at all? The Royalty would be essentially a right of citizenship regardless of any wealth status and no citizen should be excluded. In practical terms, to choose between people based on need is to retain bureaucratic methods that are proving so expensive. The wealthier would be likely to be contributing high amounts of LVT on any landed property they have, and, initially they would still be paying the higher rates of income tax which would be likely to endure for some time, even given extensive reform. F.A.Hayek in *The Road to Serfdom.* acknowledged the argument of giving everyone basic financial security but wrote that it would involve change for those currently enjoying privileged security.

Rather than *central planning by bureaucrats* in the spending of the yield from taxation, a new departure would be *the individual planning by every citizen* as they handled more of the national wealth for themselves. This would encourage the *market generated economy* rather than the *centrally directed economy*. If a banking-funded CR was added to with LVT funding, the Royalty would not lead to house price inflation. It would be of greatest benefit to the poorest and would eventually enable many targeted social security benefits to be abolished. For example, government schemes give specific benefits to pensioners, such as heating and TV license allowances. These would be superseded by the regular Citizen's Royalty payment, which pensioners would then be able to spend on what they chose for themselves. A great improvement over having that decision made for them by a politician and bureaucrat.

An important aspect of the introduction of the Royalty would be education about it, and this would relate well to the attempts by government to encourage responsibility in children through general training in citizenship. The Alaska Permanent Fund website shows what can be done. To the objection that some people would allow the Royalty to slip through their fingers 'wastefully' leaving little or nothing to show for it, is to point out that citizenisation not only give the right of a Royalty, but brings responsibilities. The choices people make about spending their Royalty would be up to them because it is fundamentally *their* money. People may make 'wise' or 'foolish' decisions but they will be *their* decisions. Later on, depending on the political possibilities, the increasing size of a Citizen's Royalty would be accompanied by reduced welfare benefits. However there will always be the need to support some people to a high level throughout their lives and in no way could a Royalty be large enough for them to do without such support. The Citizen's Royalty could finance more personally-directed help for the poor in contrast to the current bureaucracy which effectively hinders it. As this happened it would indicate citizenisation to be working.

It has been estimated that in time LVT could cover the entire needs of government spending annually (Appendix C: Harrison 1998), which currently amounts to about £6700 for every person. Assuming reform and that just 10% of this was available for the Royalty at an early stage, it would, if added to the £800 mentioned earlier from banking reform, bring around £1450 for every adult and child. Funded from just the two above sources, the impact of an extra £1300 per person on the 4.3 million households who live below the 'poverty threshold' (about £8800 a year) would be significant. Compared with Child

Benefit at £806 for the first child and £538 for subsequent children, a Royalty of £1300 per family member would make a lifestyle difference for many, especially those on low incomes.

Land Value Tax *vs* Other Taxes

Most conventional methods of taxation *penalise creativity and production.* For example, a tax on purchasing (VAT) raises the price of goods, so that fewer are bought. Income Tax is an added overhead to enterprise and can be a disincentive to work.

In contrast LVT *encourages creativity and activity* concerning the thing taxed – land. Land Value Tax brings efficiency gains to the general economy especially if combined with reductions in other taxation. Due to the lowering of land costs it would have a benign effect on virtually every business and family. It has very few of the counter-productive effects which accompany conventional taxes.

If income tax eventually became unnecessary what people earned would be solely their own concern and tax returns could become obsolete. The paperwork for LVT would be very simple by comparison.

The predictable Citizen's Royalty payment

Many people are curious at the annual budget time as to just what our Chancellor of the Exchequer will announce. What amazing new wheeze will he produce like a conjuror, that has you puzzling for weeks afterwards about just what (or who) has been done? But the payment of the Royalty would be no great mystery. The growing size of the Citizen's Royalty Fund would be clear to anyone who wanted to look on the internet, as Alaskan citizen's do with their fund. The approximate amount of the Citizen's Royalty payment would be easy to calculate by simple division by the number of citizens. The fund would build, in accordance with the (politically agreed) accumulation rate, from a proportion of the various new, that is replacement, taxes. Whilst the earliest payments might perhaps be paid annually or 6 monthly, as they grew the Royalty could be paid monthly 'Citizen' specifies everyone, children included. Non-citizen freeholders would contribute Land Value Tax, but receive no Citizens Royalty. Due to the special significance of land to citizens it might be appropriate that corporate and non-citizen freeholders should pay a higher rate of Land Value Tax. Payment to infants and young people, as well as to adults, would help to introduce children to the rights and eventually the responsibilities of citizenship as would also the proxy voting for children. If the standard Royalty amount was lower for the young, and higher for the elderly, the basic 'CR' for adults could be suffixed with J for Junior, and S for Senior. Child Benefit, which is the only current non-means tested citizen's income would be denoted CRJ. A part of the state pension could be transferred to a new CRS for older people.

A current concern is the need to encourage the establishment of individual pension schemes because of the likely future shortfall of most personal pension arrangements. The Citizens Royalty would provide a small income of immediate use and thus be of help to those among the elderly who have a pension shortfall and currently need welfare benefits. It could also build a fund for the future for those who are younger. It could help individuals, families and business partners to fund the borrowing needed to start those embryo businesses that are seen as the source of future national wealth.

Local taxes: Council Tax and Business Rates

One way to introduce LVT could be to a remodel Council Tax and Business Rates. Council Tax funds local services and is loosely related to the value of the house plus land, as occupied by two people, but it is not directly proportional to property values. The tax is likely to be just over double in amount between band A and band F, whereas the related property values are four times the amount, or very much more, in some cases. Thus do those owning the higher value properties currently bear less tax proportionate to their asset, although with respect to the services used, this shows a degree of fairness. Council Tax could be split to have separate elements of tax: on the land and on the house.

The infamous Poll Tax (Community Charge) which was abolished in the early 1990's charged individuals and was unrelated to property ownership, assets or income. It necessitated registers of every citizen solely for the purpose of the tax and resulted, in some areas, in one third of the tax being uncollected either through deliberate avoidance or bureaucratic inefficiency.

The collection of Land Value Tax is much simpler since the freeholder can usually be identified quite easily. It would be necessary for every freeholder to be registered. If the owner of any plot was not forthcoming, then the state could register the land and hold it for 12 years (the usual period for such cases). Or the state might sell it, pay the tax and hold the net proceeds until within 12 years the original owner revealed themselves. Thereafter the unclaimed proceeds would be paid into the Citizen's Royalty Fund.

The registration of citizens for the Citizen's Royalty would not bring the resistance associated with the Poll Tax, because of the benefits to be gained from this 'reverse poll tax'! Identification might be based on National Insurance numbers backed by other evidence.

Whilst Council Tax pays for local services, LVT would relate to the national Citizen's Royalty, some funding of services and the replacement of conventional taxes. Therefore, it might be more appropriate to value land for LVT purposes separately from any local assessment. Council Tax relates to local democracy and a local element to the Citizen's Royalty could be related to a locally levied LVT based on the same valuation data. The Citizen's Royalty both at national and local level would bring an entirely new dimension to politics: that of *giving* everyone cash rather than solely *taking* it through taxation. Whether Council Tax was kept or not, the valuation of the *house* itself would be unnecessary for Land Tax purposes.

The citizenisation principle would return power to people and not to any level of government 'on their behalf'; unless they choose to vote their money through a more democratic process in which they are more truly engaged than they are currently with national government. A comprehensive tax reform would reduce the reach of national government and the lower levels of local government might assume more importance. Decision making could devolve down as some central money was shifted downwards, nearer the people. Planning decisions linked through LVT to a local element of the Citizen's Royalty could be part of this process.

The introduction of LVT would have to be related to the general ability to pay, and this would take into consideration the credit received through the earlier established Citizen's Royalty. Whilst those on low incomes might be either renters or freeholders, both would be in receipt of the Royalty but only the freeholders would pay LVT. Care would need to be taken so that low-income small freeholders would not be worse off through the LVT.

The actual percentage tax charged, would be levied against regular valuations of all land. Increasing LVT and similar taxes would be accompanied by decreasing conventional taxes.

Solutions to Land Value Tax 'hard cases'

The funding of the Citizen's Royalty via Land Value Tax in particular, could leave some people financially poorer, for example owners of houses with valuable land who have insufficient income to pay the LVT despite the regular extra income of the Citizen's Royalty. Would these people have to move to a cheaper home merely to pay the tax?

There are several points to be made. One result of LVT, and for some advocates, a principle aim, is to encourage the full use and development of land within its planning designation.

A freeholder might decide to build or modify their building, for sale or rent to raise income to pay the tax. The introduction of LVT and the simultaneous reduction of other taxes would mean that the modification or extension of a house would bear less VAT on the materials or architects fees, less income tax on builders wages, and so on. Thus more development would become viable.

However the development option may not be possible or desired by the owner, and the new Royalty income might not be sufficient to make up the income shortfall. A solution, say for a low income pensioner-freeholder, could be to charge that person's estate with the accumulating tax plus interest, so that the heirs would receive less and the elderly pensioner stayed put. This would accord with one of Adam Smith's 'maxims with regard to taxes' that it should be levied at the time and manner 'in which it is likely to be convenient for the contributor to pay it...when he is likely to have wherewithal to pay.' (*The Wealth of Nations, Book Five, Chapter 2. Part 2*).

There might be scope for the sale of the land itself, with its tax liability, to a third party, or to the state itself. The house owner would pay ground rent, which would then be affordable through the proceeds of the land sale. Another solution might be that members of a family could pool their own Royalties to help an elderly parent with their LVT liability.

Thus there would be several ways to enable people to stay put. However, high land value indicates a valuable asset bringing benefits which the low income occupant is enjoying beyond the reality of their finances in a new LVT scenario. Those who are 'asset rich and income poor' cannot strictly be classified as 'poor'.

LVT could be accompanied by the elimination of Inheritance Tax at least on the land value element, due to the regular taxing of the land up to the time of transfer of the estate and thereafter under new ownership. Stamp duty on land and property transactions could be reduced under LVT, otherwise this would involve the double taxation of land. Also stamp duty can be a hindrance to mobility and as such it inhibits choice.

As has been noted, the Citizen's Royalty would provide a basic subsistence similar to the benefit of working land for food, but it would not provide the asset itself which in a pastoral system includes land for housing purposes as well as for food. However LVT, as a source of the Royalty, would increase the affordability of all housing whether for purchase or rent, which would help all household budgets, even of renters, as well as bringing the benefits of home ownership to more people.

2. TAXES, HOUSES AND JOBS

Simpler taxation, cutting bureaucracy and fraud
If tax reform resulted in the early abolition of income tax most of the black economy would no longer exist, since such things as unrecorded cash payments would not matter one way or the other. With no income tax to pay, at least initially for the majority, what people earned would be their concern alone, there would be no need for an annual tax return to assess income. The only taxation paperwork for the freeholder-citizen would be the Land Value Tax demand.

Personal taxation should be eliminated before corporate taxation, since an aim of citizenisation is that people should benefit before impersonal bodies. VAT with its bureaucratic burden for businesses is a target worthy of early abolition. Internet sales across national boundaries would be of no concern to an Exchequer that was not relying on VAT. The tax planning industry, whereby those who can afford advice, choose how much tax they pay, would shrivel. Thus the purpose of tax havens would cease and such places would have a need to invest in real businesses. There would be no way to avoid Land Value Tax.

Cutting housing costs
If just half of the current 800,000 empty homes came rapidly onto the market through the effect of LVT this would have a downward effect on prices since it would represent about 2 years supply of new units in one go.

The tendency for house prices to keep rocketing away out of reach of low earners, as seen yet again in the early years of the new century, would be much reduced. But given the need for landlords to find LVT on their empty properties it might become much cheaper to rent a home compared with buying. 'Upward only rent reviews' so commonplace in commercial leases might become an historical oddity. Home owners who would normally have to part with such large amounts of income to get a foothold on the property ladder, would find they needed a smaller mortgage than expected since the land cost element would be lower. The more settled look to prices would be due principally to the release of more land having planning permission already, rather than due to a rise in new planning consents on green fields. Instead of money being locked away in land, the future destination of money usually budgeted for housing mortgages would be released into other areas of the economy.

Some people, especially recent purchasers, would find that their property finance deal was in negative equity. Their mortgage would exceed their home's value due to a general drop in land values induced by LVT as it forced more land and houses onto the market. But the prior introduction of the Citizen's Royalty would bring new income to help with payments on the now partly unsecured loan. Thus do these reforms bring solutions to many of their effects. But special arrangements and allowances might still be needed for some owners with negative equity following lower land values caused by LVT.

The empowered economy

Gradually there would be an added impetus to the economy from the 'LVT effect' as it promoted economic activity as money currently supporting high land values was diverted to more productive ends. More sustainable general economic growth is likely, as witness the example of pre-handover Hong Kong. Building and development work facilitated by LVT would increase employment in all associated trades, professions and suppliers. Almost inevitably labour costs for building would rise as the building workforce responded to the higher demand, but higher wage rates would attract an increased supply of labour which would help the industry to cope with the new work. Those owning real estate would look on development from a new taxation standpoint especially conditioned by whether they owned the land or not. They would have incentives to develop and provide more and improved accommodation in order to increase their income to pay any tax on the land value due from them.

In the longer term it would not be expected that all housing (i.e. land) prices would stop rising. People will always want to move into larger or more desirable property or better locations, and will be prepared to bid up prices, even though they would be taking on higher Land Value Tax. But it might be expected that the market would become more predictable, less volatile and move more in line with general inflation. Valuations of all land would be publicly accessible information, as is the case in Denmark which has used Land Value Taxation for many years.

It would be justifiable to take some of the yield of LVT to pay for those public benefits, the construction of which usually raises land values, such as a by-pass, or a new railway station or railway electrification. This would introduce some alternatives to pay for the funding of the transport infrastructure.

A reduction and eventual elimination of tax on dividends and on interest from deposits, could transform the pension business. This currently locks money away from the investor due to tax rules and restricts certain funds to annuity purchase on retirement. Funds would be freed up to give more choice to investors.

The Bank of England's sledgehammer

When a house price boom gets under way the Bank of England's Monetary Policy Committee might consider and considers raising general interest rates. This would be to try and prevent inflation spreading into the general economy as too many people cash-in and spend some of their higher land wealth, after refinancing to raise cash from equity release. One problem however is that usually house prices are not rising evenly across the country. Also, a raised interest rate will affect many businesses which are struggling to survive. The device of altering interest rates is rather like using a sledgehammer to crack a nut open, it can cause more problems than it solves.

Land Value Tax would dampen property price volatility directly and enable interest rates to be set more appropriately for industry and commerce. Anyone bidding to buy a property would have to take into account a regular tax charge based on the value of the land within the total cost of the property, and this would moderate house price volatility at its source.

The people who try and manage our economy would find that they had two precise and effective instruments: interest rates and LVT, each one appropriate to a particular task. Imagine a surgeon using a saw when the incision needed a scalpel!

---

3. LOCAL CHOICES ON PLANNING

At the introduction of Land Value Taxation, it would be vital for that environmental and planning issues to be taken into account. The current policy of intensifying urban development would be assisted by the introduction of LVT. But the negative effects of this are likely to be: less-green and more crowded towns and cities; less choice of housing type; higher rise buildings less conducive to good personal interaction; smaller private gardens; and the forcing up of prices of more desirable housing despite the higher LVT on these plots. Because LVT would accelerate these trends there is a strong case for *lowering* new housing densities in urban areas on the introduction LVT, in order to extend housing choice and promote greener towns. But whatever the maximum density of the policy, LVT will always work towards this maximum as freeholders act in their own financial self-interest and develop to gain income to cover their tax liability.

The NIMBY's have a good case

The NIMBY (Not In My Back Yard) attitude is partly due to loss of amenity and also to the fear of loss of property values due to development blight. A local Royalty payment could be a monetary compensation for such loss.

An amount within the Citizen's Royalty funded from the LVT yield from a new development could be paid out locally for a limited period following the new work. Existing residents suffering from particularly high development activity would thus be compensated for its impact.

This would enable choices to be made by local communities about the amount and intensity of development they wanted. Perhaps a referendum could gauge support for the choice between various densities, or numbers, of new dwellings with a corresponding extra local Citizen's Royalty based upon a proportion of the yield of the LVT from the new development. It would be citizenisation in action.

It could ease the way for some new developments, or preserve areas,
according to local choice.

At the same time that LVT was helping to carry out the urban intensification policy, it could give incentive to rural freeholders to claim the same right to develop their building plots in order to help with the payment of *their* LVT. It is acknowledged that building on *some* green fields, has to continue in order to fulfil housing needs, but a compromise at these inevitable town and village edge-developments would be to encourage low density development there. This would help provide the numbers of dwellings needed overall in a more acceptable manner.

Citizenisation involves the taking into consideration of the preferences of as many people as possible and the handling of housing densities more flexibly. The environmental and social needs of town and rural dwellers should be taken into account and not only, as now the empty landscape lobby. The slow phasing of new, low density, edge-developments would ease the new building into the empty landscape at an acceptable pace.

The history of the bungled attempts to introduce some form of Land Tax over earlier decades shows how, unless the tax is well thought out it might cause development to dry up (see panel: *How not to tax land*). The expectation could arise, as it has done before, that the next government will abolish the tax, and developers might refrain from applying for Planning Permission, awaiting that day. If it was directly linked to the payment of a Citizen's Royalty along with reductions of other taxes these could be incentives enough to ensure its permanent acceptability by all parties. After all, who has seriously suggested that Child Benefit, the first citizen's income to date, should be abandoned?

4. NEW AND CONTINUING BENEFITS

A Citizen's Royalty could not of itself replace all the welfare needs of the very poorest and most disadvantaged, just as the Mosaic model required extra help for the poor other than free land and free credit rights. Thus state spending and provision would need to continue, but would eventually be on a reducing scale given the more efficient economy as a result of LVT replacing taxes on production etc. There is also scope for diverting spending back directly to citizens, either through further reductions in conventional taxes or in an increased Royalty payment, so that people were given the choice to purchase services directly. How big the state should be, and what it should provide, and whether some of it should be paid for at the point of use is a discussion that will no doubt continue for decades. If individuals rather than by politicians and bureaucrats make decisions on the spending of the funds entering the system market pressure would come to some service provision.

Citizenisation through the device of the Royalty would help to unite people across the nation, where current trends would separate. Imbalances of wealth whether geographical or social would moderate. The citizen's viewpoint should be kept paramount at all times. Financial statistics, taxes and costs and so on should be presented as far as possible related to the individual. For instance the cost of the NHS per person per year is around £1100. The cost of all government spending is around £6700, per person per year.

*

5. NETWORKS, RHYTHMS AND
THE LONG TERM VIEW

Networks

Human networks are flexible which enables them to absorb shocks. Rigid hierarchies that are often found in business life need regular modification to keep them working efficiently. Networks enable people to respond rapidly to change. Policies that help people to use their existing natural networks or from new ones should be encouraged.

For the fortunate who are already fulfilled in, and fairly compensated for their employment, the CR would make very little difference to their lifestyle, but for many others the new choices that even a minimal citizen's income could bring, would be empowering. Not that such benefits should be equated with mere selfishness. The opportunity for families to care for their own, whether it be the elderly or small children, rather than take paid work and employ carers, would be invaluable to many and to society generally. Life for millions of people would take on new qualities based on new choices. Young people would be encouraged to train and study in contrast to a trend now evident where some are leaving further education because of inadequate income. Mature people too would have the choice of becoming students.

The Citizens Royalty in directing funds *to the citizen* rather than *to the state for the citizen*, would increase choice. For poor families the difference will be most marked. Apart from the benefit of the non-means tested money of the CR, and lower housing costs through LVT effects, they would have the choice to take a part-time job, to do voluntary work, to study or attend training, or to start a small business. All without the financial penalty of lost benefits of the current poverty trap. The need to be *employed* full-time, may start to be replaced with a more human activity to be *creative,* carrying out fulfilling, personal, family, and other social activity. The proceeds of the Royalty and the part-time work would make these alternatives possible. This could reactivate relationships through the natural networks of family, friends, and local and special interest groups and bring many beneficial effects, far beyond merely economic ones.

Rhythms

Many people would find that they were able to choose to take recreational and restorative breaks, making for a more flexible lifestyle. The pay for some of the least desirable jobs, such as those involving unsocial hours, like weekend working and night shifts, might have to be raised. The extra security flowing from the Royalty payments could be enough for the poorest, who take such jobs, to choose not to continue doing them at the same pay.

The efforts of unions and other groups proved futile to stop the exploitation of the poor through Sunday trading. If the people taking these jobs - among the lowest paid - find that not only are their low incomes increased through the Royalty, but that their housing costs are lowered through LVT effects, they will have the choice to decide for themselves whether they take such work. Thus it is possible that a society-wide rest day could return. The ancient Jubilee cry of 'Freedom' (Chapter 2) would have a small but real echo in such a change. The prospect of the poorest becoming more able to bargain about their employment terms because of their Royalty-induced security, would help to reduce the power of the normal hierarchical business arrangement that can be oppressive, given the power differences within hierarchies. Cooperation arising from network style relationships between people who are more equal, might grow.

Sabbatical leave is not uncommon today, especially among professionals, such that after several years work for an employer, six months or a year is taken as recreational holiday or for alternative employment-related activity. The term derives from the seventh year cessation of sowing and reaping featured in the Mosaic economy (Chapter 2). As seen in chapter 6, modern business cycles describe a period of above average economic growth that is followed by quieter periods. To accept and embrace this natural rhythm could mean that more people might choose to take long breaks during recessions or at times to suit themselves because they had saved their Citizen's Royalty in earlier years. It seems possible that the introduction of LVT and banking reform might reduce the frenetic volatility of our modern economy, but J.M.Keynes' advice to raise government expenditure at such times, might see the Royalty being increased in amount, to provide general welfare directly to the citizen and to boost economic activity through citizens' spending of their Royalty. The chance of a break as a celebratory time involving debt forgiveness and *employment release,* (Chapter 2) was so different to the feared *unemployment* that occurs in the recessions, at about the same interval, in our unplanned business cycles. Is anything like this possible in our times? After all, those who are better off and those who are employed by prosperous organizations and businesses take sabbaticals, who else might not make similar choices if they had the income to cover their basic needs?

Family voting rights - the long view
Voting figures indicate that the rising generation is little interested in parliamentary politics. Maybe they are disaffected with every foible, twist and spin of their political masters. The voting habit may be still ingrained for the parents despite the apathy, but the children do not seem to be picking it up. This is a worrying trend for democracy since the fewer the participating voters the more the apathy will feed back on itself, as decisions are made that will eventually relate more heavily towards those who bother to make their presence felt. In the cause of citizenisation the Royalty would almost certainly bring renewed interest.

A useful innovation for the promotion of democracy, and in line with government encouragement of citizenship would be voting rights for children. A parent would hold a part-vote, say 1/10, 1/5 or ¼ vote, by proxy, for their child under voting age, and would cast it according to their own decision; or as the child wished as they were able to understand. This would help young people to grasp early on that their views will be increasingly important in time to come. The concept of proxy votes for children, probably sounds as bizarre to modern ears as the concept of votes for women was 100 years ago, and that of votes for all men 100 years before then. But children's voting rights would start to engage them in the democratic process bringing something of the longer term view of life that was discussed in chapter 2. After all, many decisions made today, will more intensely affect the next generation than the current one that is making the changes.

6. ASSETS AND ENTREPRENEURS

In South Africa, help is targeted through the National Empowerment Fund set up under Nelson Mandela, whereby 10% of privatisation proceeds are earmarked for black entrepreneurs to create new businesses. In the UK, the Prince's Trust has for over 20 years helped many young people's small businesses to be set up with grants but it was only in 2002 that it started to receive funding support from government. Some of the funds that are so available to support large failing businesses would be better in the long term spent on such small business start-ups – of all age groups. As has been mentioned the income in the form of a Citizen's Royalty does not provide an asset for financial independence and accommodation as land did in that pastoral society. It does not create the 'start condition' of the Mosaic system which was to be the 'return condition' after fifty years. For us the cost of providing assets, to launch a business or acquire a dwelling, unless they are inherited, will usually be through borrowing capital, the charges for which will be a substantial proportion of earnings over many years. But the Royalty could be used to finance a loan and could in a small way give access to the assets needed for a new business, which would promote further the independence and freedom essential to the aims of citizenisation.

A fund for entrepreneurs could be set up to receive some of the revenue from LVT and Banking Reform, etc., and grants made from it to nurture new businesses at the level of the individual citizen. A new Entrepreneurs Fund, alongside the Citizen's Royalty Fund could make Entrepreneurs Fund Grants. A recent idea, the Individual Learning Account (launched and withdrawn within two years) whereby everyone over 18 was entitled to receive up to £200 of training each year was a promising scheme for citizen empowerment that has Free Lunch characteristics. The easy access to education and training is no less fundamental to citizen's empowerment as access to a basic income. Although this idea was helpful, it needs seeing in the context of the deluge of new regulations annually. The number of 4642 for the year 2001 was itself up 20% from the previous year, and is a reminder of the way that government, from within and from outside national borders impinges on the lives of the citizens at many levels.

Give and take, government style

The UK government (New Labour in 2001) introduced the idea of a Baby Bond to each newborn child that might give a one off payment of about £800 for a young adult at 18 years (or £1660 if they are from a poorer family – note the inevitable means test). This amount is quite derisory compared with its likely value (unless inflation-proofed) after 18 years, but is an interesting idea which contains perhaps a seed of the principle of providing core assets for individuals. But it needs to be taken in comparison with the £5.0bn taken *annually* from pensioners through the elimination of a time-honoured tax relief in the first New Labour budget. This effectively reduced pensions by 20% on average, that is several hundred, or thousands of pounds a year. With students expected to pay high college fees at about the age they would receive the matured fund, this Baby Bond wins a very small

prize for effectiveness and can hardly be worth the cost of setting it up
at its current amount. Given the current apathy of young people about
politics it might win some votes when the babies become voters in
years to come. At best it shows how difficult it is going to be to
provide anything of real value for the ordinary citizen as long as
radically different ways of running our affairs are not found.

7. CITIZENISATION:
TOWARDS THE PRIVATISATION OF POLITICS

The model of Chapter 2 demonstrates some ancient political wisdom
concerning freedom and fairness. Despite the immeasurable advance
in technology and in material progress since, it is clear that our
political system does not offer the freedoms of those times. This might
perhaps be acceptable if it could be seen that restricted freedom is
necessary to reduce poverty. But clearly, too many poor are still with
us, and likely to remain so, given the failure *in relatively good times* to
improve matters. Freedom and fairness for us are by comparison,
goals to be reached.

For as long as the state is receiving large proportions of our
earnings, by taxing our productivity and creativity so heavily, and for
as long as privatisations of state industries merely enrich the better off,
so will the freedoms that we could exercise individually be limited.
Responsibilities with few rights are the characteristic of a slave
relationship.

The hope is that we might move towards a more equal situation
where *all* would have more resources to live their lives more to their
own choosing with less interference from the state. Hopefully this
book has shown that such an idea is not a crazy utopian dream but has
the promise of being a practical possibility; even if the idea of regular
asset restoration needs further development.

Currently the citizen's relationships with the state can preclude
some helpful relationships between people. If the state were to reduce
its intrusive reach, as the idea of subsidiarity demands, so would our
capacity increase to take more control over our own lives, and to build
new constructive relationships with each other.

To those who would want a blueprint or layout from this book for
a new *system*, the response is that what is being discussed is a *less
predictable system, because a less centrally planned system.* Once the
basic income through the Royalty was established and growing, along

with further measures to promote citizenisation, people would have more scope to arrange things as best suited them. A blueprint suggests rigidity. If citizenisation increases, many more people will find that they can be more creative and this implies flexibility. It is a conflict in terms to think that the outcomes of citizenisation can be *planned*. But you could detect that citizenisation was taking place as brand new solutions to old problems emerged as newly empowered people decided to tackle things that they never tackled before, or do things in ways that were not possible before.

Citizenisation:
Be your own politician

- the empowerment of citizens, bringing greater choice and financial security
- more entrepreneurial activity
- reduced housing costs for all
- simplicity in welfare and taxation
- increased and steadier growth for the national economy
- less intrusive bureaucracy and greater privacy of personal earnings
- the elimination of the black economy and the need for tax havens

---

Although the overall result might be less predictable than at present, any apparent uncertainty or inherent unpredictability (to those who think in terms of the planning of state affairs) it would be balanced by extra security for those usually most at risk, the poorer. Those who would expect chaos if government were to be smaller than present, exhibit a lack of faith in the capabilities of ordinary people to make responsible decisions when given basic rights. It should be possible to introduce a Citizen's Royalty early in a Parliament and to have a fully running, LVT system adding to the funding of the Royalty by its end. The logistics are not insuperable, given the political will.

To those who want more 'freedom', with no special devices to protect the weak and less favoured, then the Lottery Principle will be their guiding light. If they are currently financially favoured themselves then all may be well for them. But the arguments of these pages will have failed if they have not shown that such a society based on the workings of the Lottery Principle, promoting as it does, more freedom for the favoured, will be regressive. Treasured 'freedoms' can fade for anyone and the system may work against the favoured of the past, as their fortunes change.

Many of the ideas covered in this book have been around for

decades, as separate issues. LVT reform and citizen's income, for example, have been advocated separately, and supporters of each have been fighting their own corners with limited effect, and it is vital that they be inextricably linked together. The first without the second would be politically very difficult to introduce because of its wide reach without obvious benefit. The second without the first would merely exaggerate the poverty-engendering tendencies of the land/housing market and thus defeat its purpose in relieving poverty. But these issues can come together and form part of a bigger vision. under the general heading of what is here called citizenisation.

The interest in the raising of government income through the auction of the new 3-G mobile phone licences of recent years is minor compared with the fascination if the proceeds had generated income to every citizen. As mentioned in Chapter 4, the auction of the 3-G licences could have brought £1500 to a family of four! But nothing so imaginative was done, it was all dropped into the government money pot as mere credits for the centrally inspired spending machine, when it could have been the start of a new citizenisation theme.

The issue of the Citizen's Royalty needs to become as important in our time as the universal franchise was over 100 years ago. The socialist experiment has failed but state costs linger on, little affected by the adjustments of the right that followed. The decades pass and governments achieve little to relieve lasting poverty.

Of particular concern is the continuing division of our society with reference to real estate property. We are, economically speaking, two nations comprising: Citizen-Freeholders and Citizen-Renters. The hope is that homeowners will look beyond their somewhat uncertain property 'gains', and see that these are of less benefit than they imagined, especially when they consider the expense of their children's property solutions. Those parents who are having to help their children purchase homes of their own, may for their and other people's children's sake see the attraction of immediate income *and* lower housing costs for all. The fact that their own sizeable equity gains would drop as they were recycled to make the whole operation work, is a price to pay. However it may be considered worthwhile if it enables their children to be able to set up home without the current high costs and uncertainties both of buying and of renting. The majority of homeowners should face the fact that their equity gains will be of little financial benefit to them in their lifetime. Such an appeal to family and self-interest could be the key to the introduction of the reforms discussed, which would bring greater 'fair play' to the struggling poor as well, who are almost always renters and as such are mere spectators of the housing equity game that so many other people are playing.

International Free Lunches?

The plight of developing counties demonstrates that the Lottery Principle has been working from time immemorial internationally just as it has within national boundaries. The thesis of this book is that the only way to bring a radical new fairness is to ensure a sharing of the Free Lunches that exist in every country on the planet.

Debt forgiveness is an ancient principle, but do the economic conditions that accompany it merely impose on sovereign countries a version of capitalism and state management fashioned in the image of the debt forgivers? Do they do little more than lead to dictators opening bank accounts within safe western economies?

Firstly the citizenisation idea must take root within national boundaries, backed by a Citizen's Royalty funded from society-inspired and naturally occurring wealth. The covering of the cost of the registration of land prior to charging Land Value Tax could be a better form of aid than many current aid schemes. Following a widespread adoption of such reformed taxation in many countries, there is then a chance that ways of sharing International Free Lunches might be found.

Regulation and ad-hoc government, whether nationally or from Brussels, is often merely trying to moderate capitalistic practices and can be counterproductive. It may actually kill the golden goose, as businesses fail, succumbing to the market, hindered too by high taxes and the time cost that demands that staff spend hours wandering in bureaucratic mazes built of new regulations, tax collection and benefit administration. As noted, the Mosaic system was also based on regulation but it was of quite a different order. It included measures to ensure that everyone had resources to which they *returned* so that they could manage their own lives. By contrast the modern state machine ensures that it *retains* our resources as it attempts to increasingly micro-manage large numbers of us, as it measures the performance, delivery, targets and strategy, of every nurse, teacher, doctor, policeman, care worker, and many others. Who would have thought that professionals would need such fussy monitoring? Yet many of our regulatory devices appear merely to measure symptoms with little promise of attacking the disease. Side effects of the treatment keep emerging which require yet more regulation. Some professionals endure the bureaucratic frustration for a while and then move on to more satisfying occupations. Businesses on the edge of profitability may fold under the pressure of the demands; others may depart to more favourable tax and regulation regimes around the world, seeking out the easiest and cheapest place to make, and to keep, their profits. Tax revenue leaks away as business relocates, and governments try increasingly to hide their tax gathering from voters as they attempt to increase it from those that remain.

Downheavals:
Changes for the better

Reorganization, change and the associated upheaval is a factor of modern life. The problem is that some changes either fail to bring overall improvement, or else result in deterioration. Citizenisation as an idea involves change but the emphasis is on change which brings *simpler ways, and less complexity and releases individuals to greater freedom.* 'Downheaval' could be coined to indicate positive and welcome change.

Examples of 'downheavals' abound due to technological progress. One change is that in personal communications over the last 100 years. In the late 1800s relays of morse-code operators were needed to send messages across a continent. Now, mobile phones enable people to chat worldwide with no human intervention. Whilst change was uncomfortable for redundant telegraph operators, no one would deny the overall benefits that have flowed since.

Many government initiatives involve new regulation, complex form filling and burdensome bureaucracy and often fail to work as intended. They are mostly upheavals. The Citizens Royalty and associated tax simplification would achieve real welfare gains for the poorest and abolish the need for much cumbersome bureaucracy.

Whilst the whole world has reaped the technological benefits that the industrial revolution heralded over two hundred years ago, in terms of economics the scene is quite different. At the very same time that modern technology were gathering pace, the insights of Adam Smith and David Ricardo were known, with regards to the beneficial effects of using land values for the public good. But the failure to take these insights seriously, has resulted in the continuing endurance of poverty, despite the technological advances. The working and re-working of state economics over the decades seems highly complex and yet is uncertain and crude in outcome – a classic case of change marked mostly by upheaval.

The benefits of moving taxation away from production and labour (e.g. VAT and Income Tax) to resources (e.g. Land Value) are still taught to students of economics but, amazingly, ignored thereafter. When are we going to embrace such a beneficial 'downheaval'?

Do we truly understand the possibilities that could be released by the principles explained by Adam Smith and others about taxing land? The planning system diverts wealth to freeholders, excluding others.

The workings of the land market are against the free market philosophy and this restricts the freedom of low earners.

The Citizens Royalty combined with LVT has great appeal as a workable new solution in the fight against poverty and against the counterproductive speculation that characterises the housing market.

People are being turned off traditional politics, yet those who are not ordinarily politically active are now increasingly prepared to stand, march and protest for things that they do believe in, whether it be fuel prices or rural issues, showing that apathy is not the same as docility. Citizens need, and must, increasingly take centre stage in their own lives, starting with new economic and political rights.

Citizenisation as a theme backed with the Citizen's Royalty would indicate that politicians really wanted subsidiarity to work. To give money to citizens asking them to make decisions for themselves with it, defines subsidiarity. After all, how more local can you get than the individual citizen?

Merely to use Banking Reform and Land Value Taxation as new ways to raise extra revenue for national or European government, would be to miss the opportunity of bringing a new creative dynamic into the economy and society, through giving people more power. That this taxation reform might also eventually enable a reduction in the overall tax level is another promising outcome.

What sort of citizen?

We are already citizens, how could it mean more than it does ?

Citizenisation means that citizen choice should be more the focus of politics. It implies the acknowledgement of particular rights for people, and the expectation of new responsibilities from them.

The Citizen's Royalty is essential if citizenisation is to have any more meaning than the latest soundbite

Socialism plans for citizens, but citizenisation enables citizens to plan

---

A Citizen Royalty to everyone without means test, is the starting place to indicate a government in earnest about changing from a centralized society to a citizen-centred one. We need governments to believe less in themselves and to find ways of shedding their power to the citizen, the family and the multiplicity of groupings that make up a free society in order that it might become a fairer one. This is not so much an anti-government idea as a pro-citizen one. A new government mindset is needed which declares that government cannot know the solutions to individual's problems; that it no longer wants to pretend that it does; that it is there to empower citizens; that it will simplify taxation; and that it will acknowledge citizen's basic financial rights by establishing a Citizen's Royalty.

Citizenisation entails the increasing *privatisation of politics,* with new financial rights acknowledged for individuals, and power reduced at the centre and moved to be more local to the citizen. Thus would individuals, their families and whatever other groupings they formed themselves into, start to transform our society by doing what they decided was appropriate to them. This book has only scratched the surface of some possibilities. As people are gradually given financial resources, enjoy new rights and take on new responsibilities, many remote bureaucratic ways and oppressive styles should diminish. Many more people need to make their own successes, and their own mistakes, but they need the resources for this.

If these things start to happen, then the hope within the allegory of The Restaurant, with which this book began, might start to become a reality for many more of us, as society reshaped itself towards that elusive goal of fairness with freedom.

* * *

APPENDICES

APPENDIX A

HOUSE AND LAND COST DETAILS

Land designated for agricultural use is currently (2002) worth around £2000 per acre. Based on its agricultural value, a plot of land the size normal for building one house set in a small garden is £200 (i.e. at a rate of 10 houses per acre). But given the grant of Planning Permission for house-building, the land value of that same plot can soar from £200 to £30,000 or much more (a multiple of 150 times). A developer will readily pay £300,000 per acre for such land and inevitably this cost is reflected in the 'house' price. The cost of a house at £90,000, might have a land value within it of say £30,000. The remainder is made up of: the cost of the building (labour, 'bricks and mortar', fees, builders supervision and profit, etc, making up the balance of £60,000). This for a house of 90 square metres gross floor area.

Let us say that a buyer takes out a mortgage for the full amount of £90,000 for 25 years. The cost of interest at 5.0% in real terms, over the life of a repayment mortgage would be about £68,000 giving a total of £158,000.

This table shows how the various costs add up for a homebuyer and compares them with the homebuyer's initial income, at the beginning of the mortgage, of £20,000:

The total purchase price of £90,000 is made up of A+B+E. Interest costs are C+F

A.Land before planning permission £ 200		
B.Land after planning permission £29,800		
C.Interest on A+B <u>£22,500</u>		
D. Cost of A+B+C	£ 52,500	(2.6 years of initial income)
E.Building costs	£60,000	(3.0 years of initial income)
F. Cost of interest on E	<u>£45,200</u>	(2.3 years of initial income)
G. Cost of E+F	<u>£105,200</u>	(5.3 years of initial income)
H. Total cost over 25 years D+G	£157,700	(7.9 years of initial income)

Table (i): House and land purchase costs: 25 year period

The total cost over the mortgage period of the land-with-planning-permission element, plus interest (D), is about 2.6 years of the initial income (£20,000 p.a.); that is, about 1 year of gross income every 10 years. Regarded annually it is £2,100 p.a. - about 11% of initial gross income.

Item B, the cost of the land with planning permission, is what rises rapidly in a 'housing' price boom and drops when the market crashes. The value of the *building* is always *falling* because deterioration means that repairs are always needed. These maintenance costs for a house can be at least £6 per metre per annum (non-DIY), so the 90 square metre house might need £540 pa expenditure on average over the years to keep its value up (£45 per month: item S).

However if the building itself is extended or improved, its value in the market will rise to the amount of the expenditure, as long as the improvements are in line with what might be expected for the area. Because land prices in a boom rise so fast, their rise in value can mask the high costs of some building improvements which are in excess of what is usual for the house or the area. On resale the owners *might* recoup these costs if the land value of the plot that the house sits on has risen enough to cover them.

Land Value Tax would only be related to the land value. A house might be extended and let out to help pay the (unchanged) LVT. Thus does LVT positively *encourage* development and the provision of housing on *existing* sites. This is in contrast to Council Tax and Business Rates which rise as sites are developed. This *discourages* development on existing sites and adds to pressure on green fields for developments such as housing.

The £90,000 purchase price would be paid for by 300 monthly mortgage payments of £527 over 25 years which can be analysed as follows (to the nearest £1):

Land & interest on land costs
J. Cost of land at agricultural value: A table (i)   £   1
K. Cost of land for building: B table (i)   £ 100
L. Cost of interest on land: C table (i)   £ 75
    M. Total land and interest costs: D table (i)   £ 176 per month
Building & interest on building costs
N. Cost of the building: E table (i)   £ 200
P. Cost of interest on the building: F table (i)   £ 151
    Q. Total building and interest costs: G table (i)   £ 351
    R. Total payments: H table (i)   £ 527 per month

S. Maintenance costs (see text)   £ 45 per month

Table (ii): Monthly mortgage and maintenance analysis

APPENDIX B

TAX REFORM PROGRAMME

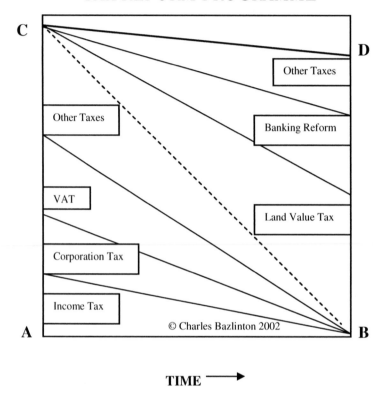

TIME →

Notional and simplified diagram of Taxation Reform

1. *The illustration shows conventional taxes (underneath the dashed line CB) diminishing with time; and resource-based taxes (above the line CB) increasing over time).*
2. *Total taxation is shown declining over time (BD is smaller than AC). This is because the new sources of tax are likely to result in a more productive economy and a reduced need for government spending on welfare, etc.*

APPENDIX C
ABBREVIATIONS, REFERENCES & SOURCES

Abbreviations

LVT Land Value Tax (also known as Site Value Tax/Rating)
CR Citizen's Royalty, The Royalty, (also known as Basic Income, Universal Benefit, National Dividend)
CRF Citizen's Royalty Fund. The fund that would receive proceeds from resources (such as land) which were to distributed to citizens through the Citizen's Royalty

Organizations and Websites

The Alaska Permanent Fund **www.apfc.org**
The website gives details on the working of the fund, payments to citizens, the composition and daily value of the share and bond portfolio, education material, etc.

The Citizen's Income Trust **www.ownbase.org.uk/citizens-income**
The Citizen's Income Trust (a UK organization) advocates a Citizen's Income (also known as Basic Income, Universal Benefit, National Dividend, and in this book Citizen's Royalty). The Trust's website gives a history of the idea and a series of questions and answers.

The Henry George Foundation (UK) **www.hgf.org**
The Henry George Foundation publishes a quarterly magazine *Land and Liberty.*

The New Economics Foundation **www.neweconomics.org.uk.**
See: Books, below

The Prince's Trust **www.princes-trust.org.uk**
The Prince's Trust exists to help young people fulfil their potential.

World Taxpayers Association **www.worldtaxpayers.org**
This campaigns for lower taxes, less waste, accountable government and taxpayers rights. It has useful summaries of taxation in many countries.

The Scott Bader Commonwealth **www.scottbader.com**
Various 'radical companies' form this group which has its well-being
entrusted to those who work in it.

Books

The quotation from Henry George's book *Progress and Poverty* in the
forward of this book is on pp. 319-320 of the 1992 reprint edition
available from Shepheard-Walwyn the principal UK publisher on
LVT and associated topics. Fred Harrison's *The Power in the Land*
(Shepheard Walwyn 1983) and his latest *Boom Bust* (Shepheard-
Walwyn 2005) are highly regarded expositions on LVT. Harrison is
also editor of *The Losses of Nations*, (Othila Press, 1998) which
covers Public Rent Dividends (such as Land Tax and others) in several
countries and gives economic data. *Standing for Justice,* John Stewart
(Shepheard-Walwyn 2001) is the biography of Andrew Maclaren MP,
who campaigned for Land Value Tax reform during the last century.
Land Value Taxation Around The World. Ed. Robert V. Andelson
(Blackwell 3rd edition) is an historical survey of five continents.
Creating New Money. Joseph Huber and James Robertson (New
Economics Foundation 2000), explains how money is created and the
interaction between banks, the government, businesses and citizens,
with suggestions for reform which could lead to cuts in conventional
taxes and the introduction of a Citizen's Income. It contains a
reference to the 'the free lunch' that commercial banks receive. *The
New Economics of Sustainable Development,* James Robertson
(European Commission and Kogan Page 1999) explores a wide range
of socio-economic, development and financial issues
The Douglas Manual Philip Mairet. (Stanley Nott 1934), is a summary
of excerpts from the writings of C.H.Douglas who campaigned for
banking reform during the 1920's and 1930's and advocated a
National Dividend for all citizens.

Other books:
Capitalism with a Human Face Samuel Brittan (Ed. Elgar 1995)
Japan. The Coming Collapse Brian Reading (Orion 1992)
The Trouble with Prosperity James Grant (Wiley 1996)
The Road to Serfdom F.A.Hayek (Routledge 1946 Abr. Edition)
The Wealth of Nations Adam Smith (1776)
Essays in Land Economics V.H.Blundell (Econ & S. S.Res.Ass.1993)
Privatising Public Enterprises Graham & Prosser (Clarendon 1991)

Dictionary of Economics Bannock, Baxter & Davis (Penguin 1992)
A Dictionary of Sociology Gordon Marshall (Oxford 1998)

Bible references for Chapter 2: (not exhaustive*)* The Mosaic law: Exodus (chapters) 20-23, Deuteronomy 5-31. The phrase 'love your neighbour as yourself': *Leviticus 19.* Outcomes to be expected from law observance: *Lev. 26, Deut. 28.* Legal and political arrangements: *Ex.18, Numbers 11, Deut. 16-17.* Land: *Lev. 25.* Time cycles: *Ex.15, 20-21, Deut. 5.* Free food: *Deut. 23.* Gleaning: *Ex.23, Lev.19,23, Deut. 24.* Loans and Interest: *Ex. 22, Lev. 25, Deut.23.* Employment: *Ex. 21, Lev.25, Deut. 15.* Tithing: *Lev.27, Num.18, Deut. 12,14,26.* Education: *Deut.6,31.* Gibeah / Mizpah: *Judges 19-21.* Camel swallowing: *Matthew 23.* Jesus and the cornfield incident: *Matt.12.*

*

INDEX

mobile phone licences 150
Mohammed 13
- *see also* Islam
monarchy in ancient Israel 28-9
Monetary Policy Committee 141
monopolies
- high earnings as 123
- land & housing market 7, 52-3
mortgage **62**, **156**
Mosaic system
- anti-monopoly measures 25
- asset restoration 31
- building regulations 14
- Commandments, The Ten 14
- central authority, aspects of 13, 19, 27
- celebration 13, **20**, 96-7, 144-6
- charity 23
- day of rest 115-16
- debt 24-5
- debt forgiveness 24-5, 27, 101
- economic rent 26, 41, 54
- economy as a game 11-12, 33, 96
- education 29
- egalitarian features 21
- employment 19, 26-7, 112, 119
- ethical aspects 15-16
- family tenure **18**, 107
- foreigners 19
- free food 23
- gleaning 23-4
- interest ban 24, 43
- Jubilee year 18, **20**, 41,102
- land 18-21
  - allocation 19
  - freeholding in perpetuity 20, 25-6
  - redemption 25-6
  - sale 20, 25-6
  - valuation 20, 25-6
- legal (and law) 19, 27
- Levites 19, 27
- life, quality of 16
- life, sanctity of 16
- loans 24-5
- Lottery Principle 6-7, 12, 31

- monopoly 25
- networks 18
- political 19, 27-9, 38
- recovery after failure 22, 28
- relationships 14, 23, 107-9
- rests 20, 95-6, 115-16
- safety wall 14
- slavery *see* employment
- time cycles 19-23, **20**, 103, 111
- tithe 24
- welfare 23-5
- *see also* Judges
Moses **17**
- economist, political scientist 11, 17
- *see also* Mosaic System
Muslims 11
Mutality 102, 124

Naomi 28
National Benefit
  see Citizen's Royalty
National Dividend 39-41, 58-9
  -*see also* Citizen's Royalty
National Empowerment Fund
  see South Africa
National Health Service (NHS)
  126, 129, 143
National Lottery, The 4
nationalisation 5, 130
- land **63**, **66**
negative equity 56, 140
negative income tax 35
national insurance *see* taxation
networks 18, 56, 79, 107-11, 144
network marketing 108
New Economics of Sustainable Development, The 39, 160
New Labour 147, 160
NIMBY (Not In My Back Yard)
  76, 81, 84, **142**
noise 81

oil 2-4, 47
on-line sales 139
OPEC 114

This book is available through
mail order or your local bookshop
or visit: www.the-free-lunch.com

Mail order
Send a cheque or postal order made
payable to:

Orchard Four Books
PO Box 103
Alresford
Hants
SO24 9XN
UK

UK Orders:
Add £2.00 for postage and
packing for the first book and
£1.50 per additional book sent
to the same address in the UK

Overseas orders:
Add postage for 320gm per book
and **either** the equivalent to £5
handling fee per *order* **or** £1if
paying with £ sterling

PLEASE PHOTOCOPY THIS FORM TO ORDER

ORDER:

First book @ £ 9.99.... £   9.99
P & P   @ £ 2.00.... £   2.00
Further copies
....@ £ 9.99 ... £.........
P & P:
.........@ £1.50 per copy £_____
Total enclosed
cheque/ PO...........**£**_____

Please allow 14 days for delivery.
Please add the delivery address if
different to payee's.
Tick the box if you do not wish to
receive any additional
information ☐

Prices and availability subject to change
without notice

YOUR DETAILS:

name...
address

....

....

....

....

....

POSTCODE........................

telephone : ....

email: ....